PEAK PERFORMANCE

Unlock the Science of Living an Extraordinary Life

By

Dr. Jason M. Merritt, PsyD

TREMENDOUS
LEADERSHIP
Leadership with a kick!

Tremendous Leadership
PO Box 267 • Boiling Springs, PA 17007
(717) 701 - 8159 • (800) 233 - 2665
www.TremendousLeadership.com

Tremendous Leadership's titles may be bulk purchased
for business or promotional use or for special sales. Please
contact Tremendous Leadership for more information.

Tremendous Leadership and its logo are trademarks of
Tremendous Leadership. All rights reserved.

Paperback ISBN: 978-1-961202-52-8
eBook ISBN: 978-1-961202-53-5

DESIGNED & PRINTED IN THE
UNITED STATES OF AMERICA

ENDORSEMENT FOR
PEAK PERFORMANCE

"Peak Performance is an expertly structured guide to personal and professional development that translates evidence-based research into practical, daily action. Dr. Merritt strikes a powerful balance between focused persistence and personal well-being, reminding readers that sustainable excellence comes not from overextension but from disciplined, intentional effort. This book challenges the myth of innate talent and instead affirms that greatness is forged through consistent, purposeful practice. With thoughtful strategies, compelling stories, and reflective prompts, Peak Performance calls us to pursue what matters most with clarity, precision, and heart."
—Dr. Marcie LePine, Ph.D.,
Clinical Professor, Organizational Behavior & Leadership Scholar, Arizona State University.

"Dr. Merritt's Peak Performance is a masterclass in achieving excellence with authenticity. Grounded in positive psychology, it blends research with reflection, offering actionable tools like SMART goals, grit, and flow to help readers align ambition with purpose. Whether you're leading a team or pursuing personal growth, this inspiring and practical guide is a must-read for thriving in school, work, and life."
—Dr. Audrey Rabas,
Senior Doctoral Research Advisor | Academic and Leadership Mentor | Applied Researcher

"*Peak Performance is packed with real-life examples and insightful analysis that clearly outline the action steps required to become your best. It is a well-written guide with practical explanations and hands-on tools that equip readers to push through adversity, build resilience, and achieve long-term mastery. This book is a must-read for students and educators alike as we work together to guide the next generation toward realizing their full potential. The sooner someone begins applying these principles in their life, the more meaningful success, fulfillment, and growth they will experience—academically, professionally, and personally.*"
—Gary Udouj, Jr., Ed.D.
Director, Career Education and District Innovation Fort Smith Public Schools

"*Dr. Jason Merritt didn't just write a book—he built a blueprint. Peak Performance gives you the science behind the grind and the soul behind the strategy. It's equal parts research, resilience, and real talk—and I absolutely loved it. If you're tired of fluff and ready to live with purpose, grit, and tremendous clarity, this is the book that will get you there.*"
—Dr. Tracey C. Jones,
USAF Veteran | Leadership Speaker | Author of *SPARK: Five Essentials to Ignite the Greatness Within*

ABSTRACT

Many wonderful books inspire us to push toward success, but they don't reveal the hidden mechanics that create success. *Peak Performance*, in contrast, unlocks the psychological engines behind extraordinary achievement, offering a research-backed roadmap to reaching your highest potential. This book clarifies the actions you should take now, and uncovers the science behind the strategies found in self-improvement books—helping you understand *why* they work and how to apply them more effectively in your own life.

This book explores three essential categories of psychological principles that determine success. The first three constructs are foundational principles—without them 94% of goal pursuits fail before gaining momentum. The next four principles are crucial for endurance, preventing another 5% of pursuits from faltering before the finish line when faced with challenging setbacks. Finally, the last five constructs separate the top 1%—those who reach true peak performance—from everyone else.

Whether you're a leader, coach, professional, athlete, or student, these evidence-based principles will help you identify blind spots, align your actions with your ambitions, and unlock extraordinary results. Unlike books that lean on personal anecdotes, *Peak Performance* lets rigorous research and inspiring stories speak for themselves, ensuring clear, actionable steps free from the author's bias. No matter where you are on your journey, this book provides proven tools to push beyond your current limitations and achieve the extraordinary with your one life.

CONTENTS

Dedication . . . . *xiii*

Acknowledgements . . . . *xv*

Welcome to Peak Performance 1

Section 1: Igniting Your Resolve..................................5
Story: Using Resolve to Break Barriers and Inspire.........5

Chapter 1 – Purpose Statement: Aligning Your Path
with Your Core Values 9
Story: Using Purpose to Revolutionize an Industry.........9
Definition of a Personal Purpose Statement..................10
The Importance of a Purpose Statement
for Peak Performance...11
Creating Your Personal Purpose Statement...................17
Personal Purpose Statement.......................................20
Chapter 1 Reflection: How Your Purpose
Statement Affects Peak Performance 21
Chapter 1 Action Items...22

Chapter 2 – Positive Psychology: Empowering Peak
Performance through Positivity 23
Story: Finding Positivity Despite the Darkness 23
Definition of Positive Psychology 24
The Importance of Positive Psychology for Peak
Performance...25
Enhancing Positivity in Your Life 33

Chapter 2 Reflection: How Your Positivity
Affects Your Peak Performance 39
Chapter 2 Action Items...40

Chapter 3 – Goal Orientation: Cultivating a Mastery
Mindset 43
Story: The Power of the Mastery Mindset 43
Definition of a Goal Orientation 44
The Importance of Goal Orientation for Peak
Performance 47
Embracing Mastery Approach in Your Life 51
Chapter 3 Reflection: How Goal-Orientation
Affects Peak Performance..58
Chapter 3 Action Items...59

Section 2 – Fueling Your Motivation.............................61
Story: Fueling Your Ambition and Drive 61

Chapter 4 – SMART Goals: Bridging Ambition and
Achievement 65
Story: SMART Goals and Determination—
Liz Murray's Incredible Journey...............................65
Definition of a SMART Goal 67
The Importance of Using SMART Goals for
Peak Performance..68
Using SMART Goals Effectively for Peak
Performance 69
Chapter 4 Reflection: Why SMART Goals are
Essential for Peak Performance 74
Chapter 4 Action Items...75

Chapter 5 – Volition: Fueling Motivation by
Harnessing Passion 77
Story: The Transformative Power of Volition.............77
Definition of Volition..78

The Importance of Volition for Peak Performance........80
Effectively Cultivating and Applying Volition
    for Peak Performance..82
Chapter 5 Reflection: The Power of Volition
    on Peak Performance 85
Chapter 5 Action Items..86

Chapter 6 – Resilience: Growing through adversity.........87
Story: Using Adversity for Extraordinary Success 87
Definition of Resilience..88
The Importance of Resilience for
    Peak Performance..89
Effectively Cultivating and Applying Resilience
    for Peak Performance..92
Chapter 6 Reflection: Why Resilience is
    Foundational for Peak Performance..........................98
Chapter 6 Action Items..99

Chapter 7 – Grit: The Backbone of Sustained Effort
    and Achievement 101
Story: The Unbreakable Spirit of John Akhwari 101
Definition of Grit 102
The Importance of Grit for Peak Performance............104
Effectively Cultivating and Applying Grit
    for Peak Performance..105
Chapter 7 Reflection: Why Grit is vital for Peak
    Performance 109
Chapter 7 Action Items..110

Section 3 – The Path to Becoming Extraordinary 113
Story: The Voice that Defied Limits 113

Chapter 8 – Flow State: Tapping into Peak
Performance Flow..117
Story: Mastering the Flow State....................................117

Definition of Flow State 118
The Importance of Flow for Peak Performance 120
Effectively Achieving the Flow State for Peak
    Performance 121
Chapter 8 Reflection: How Flow Unlocks Peak
    Performance 124
Chapter 8 Action Items..................................124

Chapter 9 – Skill Development: Cultivating Skills
to Fuel Extraordinary Success 127
Story: From Struggle to Master Surgeon 127
Definition of Skill Development 128
The Importance of Skill Development
    for Peak Performance..............................129
Effective Skill Development for Peak Performance 131
Chapter 9 Reflection: Using Skill Development to
    Generate Peak Performance 135
Chapter 9 Action Items..................................136

Chapter 10 – Automaticity: Automating Success
for Peak Performance 137
Story: The Incredible Power of Daily Habits 137
Definition of Automaticity.............................139
The Importance of Automaticity for
    Peak Performance..................................140
Effectively Developing Automaticity for Peak
    Performance 141
Chapter 10 Reflection: How Automaticity Unleashes
    Peak Performance..................................145
Chapter 10 Action Items.................................146

Chapter 11 – Goal-Congruency: Aligning Your
Resources for Maximum Success..........................149
Story: An Audacious Future through
    Goal-Congruent Behavior 149

Definition of Goal-Congruent Behavior.......................151
The Importance of Goal-Congruent Behavior for
    Peak Performance..152
Effectively Developing Goal-Congruent Behavior for
    Peak Performance..154
Chapter 11 Reflection: How Goal-Congruent
    Behavior Creates Peak Performance........................159
Chapter 11 Action Items...159

Chapter 12 – Being the Best: Pushing Past Average
to Achieve Extraordinary Success 161
Story: From Humble Beginnings to Industry
    Outlier 161
Definition of Being an Outlier 164
The Importance of Being an Outlier for Peak
    Performance 165
Effectively Becoming Your Best for Peak
    Performance 167
Chapter 12 Reflection: How Being Your Best Creates
    Peak Performance..170
Chapter 12 Action Items...171

Your Story..173
References 177
About the Author...181

DEDICATION

To my cherished children Joshua, Elizabeth, and Rebekah:

This book was written with deep love and purpose, born from a desire to gift you every insight I could gather about the psychology of peak performance. Each page reflects years of study, experience, reflection, and prayer for wisdom, meant to help you understand the path toward excellence, resilience, and meaningful achievement.

Your teachable spirits, unrelenting curiosity, love of learning, and thoughtful minds have always given me hope that you will use this knowledge to fulfill the extraordinary purposes God has placed within each of you. This book is for you, not just as a guide, but as a tribute to the incredible young people you already are.

You made sacrifices alongside me as I pursued the research and writing of this work, and you embraced the discipline and perseverance required to grow your own gifts and talents. I know these tradeoffs aren't always easy, especially at your age, but I believe with all my heart that God will honor your faith and diligence in due time.

I hope you will always remember that I am deeply proud of you and love you more than words can express. You have been the greatest blessing of my life. As long as I have strength, I will support your growth and your dreams with everything I have.

With all my love, and with our best always ahead,

Dad

ACKNOWLEDGEMENTS

With deep gratitude and sincere admiration, I want to acknowledge those whose generosity, belief, and brilliance helped bring *Peak Performance* to life.

To Dr. Tracey Jones, thank you for encouraging me to take the risk and move beyond my cautious nature—to trade in prudence for purpose, and fear for faith in what this book could become. Your confidence in both the message and the mission of this project gave me the courage to believe that the risk was worth the tradeoffs. You inspired me to shift further into my strengths of industriousness and pour myself into this endeavor. Thank you also for warmly welcoming me into the Tremendous Leadership family—an honor I carry with great pride. Your encouragement, experience, and vision added immeasurable excitement and purpose to my efforts.

To Jenn Nori, your editorial expertise elevated this project from good to truly excellent. With a meticulous eye for detail, a strong sense of style and tone, and a deep understanding of the reader's perspective, you shaped this work into its best possible form. More than that, you continually spoke words of life and faith into me—reminding me to look beyond my limitations and trust in what God can accomplish through a willing, if unlikely, vessel. Your encouragement and conviction reminded me that the work we do matters and that He always completes what He begins.

To my son, Joshua Merritt, thank you for stepping into this project without hesitation. Your contribution to the conceptual models—visually capturing and clarifying the principles woven throughout the book—was both creative and critical. Your skill in presentation, your clarity in design, and your instinct for application brought structure and insight that made these ideas far more accessible to the reader. Your work not only supported this project, it strengthened it.

Without the three of you, this book would not have reached the professional quality required to meet its readers, nor would it have crossed the finish line. I am forever grateful for your investment, your belief, and your partnership in this vision. May this work reach everywhere God intended for it to reach.

WELCOME TO
PEAK PERFORMANCE

Thank you for allowing me to join you on your journey toward achieving your very best. Your interest in peak performance speaks volumes about your commitment to growth, and I applaud both your curiosity and your effort. I am rooting for your success.

I also respect your time, which is why I have worked diligently to bring you the most accurate research on the key psychological factors that drive peak performance—while eliminating unnecessary content. While each chapter stands on its own, they also work together to create a profound overall impact on your outcomes. I recommend reading the book sequentially at first, then revisiting the areas that resonate most with you for deeper focus.

Along the way, you may uncover blind spots that would have held you back—perhaps the role of goal orientation in sustaining motivation or the impact of your work environment on your ability to focus. You will also gain deeper insight into familiar concepts like grit, positivity, and SMART goals. These constructs are powerful on their own, but when combined, they create a multiplier effect that can propel you to levels of success you never thought possible.

I encourage you to fully immerse yourself in each chapter. Step into the real-life stories that illustrate each concept.

Imagine yourself in those scenarios, recognizing where the same principles apply to your own life. As you reach the step-by-step application section of each chapter, commit to implementing even the simplest strategies. Remember, you don't have to change the world—small shifts in awareness and action can lead to surprisingly significant results in your life.

To guide you effectively, this book divides constructs into three sections:

The first section centers on *why* we pursue goals and what determines our resolve to stay engaged. In an article by Dr. Bryan Robinson in Forbes magazine, it is estimated that 94% of goals are abandoned before they can be developed into the skills needed to truly benefit others, leaving their potential for usefulness forever unrealized. Without the right foundation, even the most talented individuals fall short. The tools in this section will help you clarify your direction and solidify your commitment for the long journey ahead.

The second section focuses on the psychological constructs that sustain you when obstacles arise. Setbacks, failures, and the often lonely road to excellence can discourage even the most determined individuals. This section equips you with the mindset and strategies to push through adversity and maintain motivation—even when others see your dedication as an obsession. By applying these principles, you will find joy in the process and begin to separate yourself from the average performer.

The third section is where peak performance transforms into true mastery. This is where you move beyond competency and into the realm of outliers—those who have made every mistake possible in their field but have persisted, learned, and grown. The constructs in this section will enable you to perform at a level that others simply can't sustain. This is where your skills become so refined, so valuable, that you can contribute in ways that impact your family, your organization, and even society as a whole.

Throughout this book, I have intentionally set aside personal philosophies and opinions. My goal is to let research in goal achievement, motivation, and human flourishing do the talking. The psychological constructs presented here are not theoretical—they have been observed, studied, and proven. While your individual circumstances may shape how you apply them, the principles remain universal. With only minor adjustments, you can harness these strategies to achieve success beyond what you previously believed possible.

Writing this book has been both a privilege and a passion. I genuinely hope to play some small part in your well-lived life. I hope that what you learn here helps you reach your very best. I am proud of you, and I am vigorously cheering you on as you learn, fail, grow, and eventually change the world around you for the better.

Now, let's begin. We will start with a powerful story that illustrates the role of purpose and resolve in accomplishing the impossible. As you will see throughout this book, accomplishing what others see as impossible appears time and time again in the lives of those who achieve extraordinary success while following the psychological blueprint for peak performance.

Section 1

IGNITING YOUR RESOLVE

Igniting your purpose can reshape your life's trajectory, giving it clarity, meaning, and momentum—This is your *"why"* factor. As we begin this section, let's reflect on a remarkable story that demonstrates the transformative force of a life driven by resolve.

Story: Using Resolve to Break Barriers and Inspire

In 1954, a 25-year-old British medical student named Roger Bannister stood at a crossroads. Training to become a doctor demanded most of his energy, but he also carried a dream that many believed was impossible: to run a mile in under four minutes. For years, experts claimed that the human body simply wasn't capable of such a feat. But Roger saw things differently. It wasn't just about breaking a record for him—it was about testing the limits of human potential and inspiring others to push beyond what seemed possible.

With this goal resolved, Roger balanced rigorous medical training with grueling running sessions on his lunch breaks. He ran in all conditions—rain, wind, and exhaustion—and refined his mindset, focusing not on the barriers ahead but on the opportunity to prove that limits were meant to be shattered. On May 6, 1954, Roger stepped onto a track in Oxford, England, with a clear sense of why he was there. Fueled by his belief in what could be achieved, he crossed the finish line in 3 minutes and 59.4 seconds, becoming the first human in recorded history to break the four-minute mile.

Roger's story is often celebrated as a tale of grit and resilience, but more importantly, it's about intense personal determination. He didn't run for fame or fortune; he ran because he believed in challenging perceptions and inspiring others to reach for something greater. That sense of purpose didn't end at the finish line. After retiring from athletics, Roger dedicated his life to medicine, becoming a distinguished neurologist and continuing to push boundaries in a new field.

This story highlights the transformative power of knowing our *why*, showing how it can drive us to achieve the extraordinary, even in the face of overwhelming challenges. In this section, we'll explore the critical role that purpose plays in shaping a life of direction, meaning, and focus. Over the next three chapters, we'll uncover how to define what truly motivates you—what inspires you to give your best effort, persevere through setbacks, and overcome distractions. Without a clear and passionate sense of internal motivation, we naturally fall into a cycle of inconsistency, where obstacles and boredom derail progress and leave us feeling stuck or starting over repeatedly without seeing any meaningful progress.

This section will also focus on the power of cultivating a positive and optimistic outlook. As you move toward your goals—and even as you navigate each day—cultivating a positive mindset will help ensure you have the energy needed to keep taking the next step. This mindset will allow you to see possibilities where others see roadblocks and excuses. While all emotions play a vital role in our personal growth and balance, building a foundation of positivity is essential for achieving peak performance and overall well-being.

We'll conclude this section by exploring a powerful concept known as goal orientation. This lens helps us understand not just the environment we are operating in, but also how we choose to approach our goals internally. Our goal orientation can either propel us forward or keep us stuck, as we either seek growth or shy away from challenges in an attempt to protect our ego. Whether we're motivated by external approval, a drive to reach our full potential, or simply the need to meet basic expectations, understanding our goal orientation can be life-changing. When aligned with a clear sense of purpose and an optimistic mindset, it has the power to turn stress from a limiting obstacle into a powerful catalyst for growth— unlocking better outcomes and sustained progress over time.

As we begin, consider this: without igniting and harnessing our true purpose, we risk drifting aimlessly through the one life we have. What does this look like in reality? The statistics paint a sobering picture: each year, 30–40% of college students drop out of their degree programs, while 62.3% take six or more years to graduate.[1] Once in the workforce, the average American changes jobs 12 times over their lifetime, with an average tenure of just 4.1 years at each employer.[2] These frequent shifts often stem from dissatisfaction and a lack of fulfillment, highlighting the profound impact that a clear sense of purpose—or the absence of it— can have on our career success and overall life trajectory.[1,2]

CHAPTER 1

PURPOSE STATEMENT
ALIGNING YOUR PATH WITH YOUR CORE VALUES

STORY: USING PURPOSE TO REVOLUTIONIZE AN INDUSTRY

In the early 1900s, a young man named Clarence Saunders grew up in rural Tennessee, working tirelessly on his family sharecrop farm, at a sawmill, and at a local general store during the holidays. By age 14, Clarence was working full-time at the general store where he developed a clear sense of purpose: he wanted to revolutionize how people shopped for groceries. At the time, grocery stores operated with clerks fetching items for customers—an inefficient and frustrating system. Clarence envisioned a new approach: a store where customers could browse aisles, select items themselves, and save time and money.

Despite having only completed two years of formal education and leaving school completely at age 14, Clarence focused relentlessly on this purpose, becoming an avid reader and autodidact. At age 19, he was rapidly advancing in the wholesale grocery industry. He worked consistently, sketching designs and experimenting with layouts. In 1916, at age 35, he opened the first self-service grocery store in Memphis,

Tennessee, naming it Piggly Wiggly. His idea was simple but groundbreaking, and it changed retail forever. Within five years, there were 615 stores in 200 cities and 40 states. By 1923, there were 1,267 stores.

Clarence's success wasn't born from extraordinary intellect or resources—it stemmed from the clarity of his purpose and his consistent efforts to bring it to life. That unwavering focus helped him overcome challenges and refine his vision until it became a reality. His clarity of purpose didn't just improve his life; it sparked a retail revolution, impacting countless others.

Definition of a Personal Purpose Statement

A personal purpose statement is a psychological concept that serves as a very clear and intentional declaration of an individual's guiding principles, core values, and long-term aspirations. It is a deeply personal articulation of what you find meaningful and worth pursuing, helping individuals align their actions, goals, and decisions with their unique strengths and values.

This guiding framework brings clarity and focus, enabling us to prioritize what truly matters and approach opportunities and challenges with a clear, objective lens. Rooted in our internal values, it ignites intrinsic motivation, driving our sustained effort even in the face of inevitable setbacks. Acting as a personal compass, a purpose statement provides direction and fosters resilience during periods of uncertainty, all while reflecting our core identity and promoting authenticity and well-being. By aligning our goals with our values, talents, and strengths, it enhances engagement and commitment, offering a stabilizing force that supports consistent outcomes as we navigate stress and adversity throughout life's journey.

THE IMPORTANCE OF A PURPOSE STATEMENT
FOR PEAK PERFORMANCE

Research demonstrates that a strong sense of purpose significantly enhances our ability to manage stress and overcome adversity by fostering psychological resilience. Purpose serves as an anchor, helping us regain stability and uncover meaning even in the most challenging situations. Beyond resilience, it delivers enduring fulfillment by aligning our efforts with meaningful, impactful actions that foster personal growth and contribute to the well-being of others. This eudaimonic approach to life—centered on long-term fulfillment and deeper purpose—stands in sharp contrast to the temporary satisfaction of hedonistic pursuits of instant pleasure, which often leave us unfulfilled, distracted, and yearning for more.[3]

When developing our purpose statement, we must consider several key components. It should be clear, fueled by intrinsic motivation, and provide a sense of direction through meaningful milestones. It must align authentically with our talents, strengths, and passions, remain congruent with our goals and actions, and ultimately offer long-term fulfillment.

Clarity and Focus

A well-crafted purpose statement serves as a guiding framework that helps us prioritize what truly matters. By cutting through the noise of daily distractions, it provides a clear lens to evaluate opportunities, challenges, and decisions, ensuring that our efforts are directed toward meaningful and impactful actions. This clarity not only reduces mental clutter but also enables us to stay aligned with our values and aspirations, making our goals more tangible and achievable.

The following is an excerpt of a good example of a purpose statement that demonstrates this clarity and focus:

Empower my students through education and mentorship, fostering confidence, mastery, and hope for a brighter future.

This statement is precise, actionable, and aligned with a clear vision. This example can be further broken down into sub-goals that are measurable, such as:

- Providing one-on-one mentorship to at least 10 students per semester, focusing on building their confidence and academic mastery.
- Developing and delivering a minimum of three new educational workshops each year, designed to equip students with critical skills for personal and professional growth.
- Facilitating at least five internship or scholarship opportunities annually to help students build hope and pathways toward a brighter future.

These specific actions illustrate how clarity in a purpose statement translates into meaningful, goal-oriented steps that create a lasting impact.

In contrast, the following bad example of a purpose statement lacks focus and direction:

To help my students and be a good teacher.

This vague statement fails to inspire action or convey a clear vision. Without defined priorities or measurable objectives, it becomes difficult to evaluate progress or ensure meaningful contributions.

A strong purpose statement must go beyond generic intentions to articulate a clear framework that drives purposeful action and fosters long-term impact. When done well, it becomes a powerful tool to guide our choices, motivate consistent effort, and create value for ourselves and others.

Intrinsic Motivation

A powerful purpose statement is rooted in your internal values and deepest aspirations, serving as a wellspring of intrinsic motivation. This internal drive goes beyond external rewards or recognition; it taps into what truly matters to you, fueling a sense of passion and commitment. Intrinsic motivation becomes the essential force that sustains your effort and resilience, particularly when you face inevitable setbacks, disappointments, or challenges.

Unlike fleeting external motivators, such as accolades or material gains, intrinsic motivation creates a lasting source of energy that propels you forward, even in the absence of immediate success. It's what enables you to stay the course when the road is tough and others might give up. By aligning your purpose statement with what inspires you from within, you cultivate the emotional and psychological resources needed to push through obstacles, maintain consistency, and find meaning in your journey—regardless of the circumstances. This internal inspiration becomes the bedrock of a purpose-driven life, guiding you to persevere and thrive.

Sense of Direction

In a world abundant with distractions and competing priorities, a well-crafted purpose statement serves as your compass, offering clarity and direction amid the noise. It provides a clear sense of where you want to go and what truly matters, helping you navigate uncertainty, change, and the constant barrage of demands on your time, energy, and resources.

Without a guiding purpose, it's easy to become overwhelmed, scattered, or led astray by short-term temptations and distractions. A purpose statement focuses you, keeping you moving toward your values and aspirations. It fosters a forward-focused mindset that helps you prioritize meaningful actions over spontaneous impulses, ensuring that your energy is spent on what aligns with your larger vision for life.

This sense of direction also strengthens your resilience, allowing you to adapt and persevere when circumstances are difficult or when obstacles arise. Instead of feeling lost or defeated, your purpose keeps you oriented toward the bigger picture, reminding you why your efforts matter and helping you maintain momentum. In this way, a purpose statement isn't just a tool for achieving goals—it's a guidepost for staying true to yourself and living a life of intention and fulfillment.

Identity and Authenticity

With our noisy environments filled with endless societal pressures, it's easy to lose sight of who we are and what truly matters to us. A purpose statement anchors us in our core identity, serving as an important reminder of our values, passions, and the unique qualities that define us. This roadmap ensures that our decisions and actions remain aligned with our authentic selves, even when external pressures try to pull us in different directions.

By grounding us in our values, a purpose statement encourages us to act with integrity and consistency. This alignment not only fosters authenticity but also creates a deep sense of satisfaction and well-being. When our actions and goals are congruent with our inner selves, we feel more fulfilled and confident in our choices, knowing they reflect who we truly are.[4]

Moreover, this authenticity builds resilience against external influences—whether it's the expectations of others, peer pressure, or the allure of short-term gratification. It empowers us to resist distractions that don't align with our purpose, freeing us to pursue a life that feels meaningful and true to our aspirations.

Living authentically through the guidance of our purpose statement also strengthens our relationships and connections. When we're clear about our identity and values, we naturally attract people and opportunities that resonate with our authentic selves, creating a more enriching and supportive environment. In essence, a purpose statement doesn't just guide what we do—it defines who we are and how we live, enabling us to navigate life's complexities with confidence and clarity.

Goal-Congruency

While navigating our day-to-day responsibilities, surprise opportunities, and other distractions competing for our attention, it's easy to feel overwhelmed or pulled in conflicting directions. A purpose statement acts as our foundation, allowing us to align our efforts with our goals that truly matter to us. By defining our purpose, our goals are no longer arbitrary or driven by passing trends but are deeply connected to who we are and what we hope to achieve.

This alignment between our goals and our purpose creates a powerful sense of congruency, boosting our commitment and engagement. When we know our efforts serve a meaningful purpose, we're more likely to stay focused and persistent, even when challenges arise. Instead of chasing scattered ambitions or being sidetracked by short-term distractions, we empower ourselves to direct our energy toward objectives that truly resonate with us and contribute to our long-term growth and fulfillment.

Moreover, a purpose-driven approach ensures that we prioritize effectively, spending our time and resources on pursuits that align with our values and aspirations. This clarity not only reduces decision fatigue, but also helps us measure our progress in a way that feels authentic and rewarding. Each step forward becomes a reflection of our deeper goals, reinforcing our motivation and sense of accomplishment.

By integrating our goals with our purpose, we also cultivate a sense of direction that sustains us over the long haul. This alignment transforms goal-setting from an effortful, task-oriented exercise into a meaningful journey of self-fulfillment and impact. When our goals and purpose work hand in hand, we unlock a level of focus and excitement that propels us toward success, ensuring that our actions today build a foundation for the future we envision. Together, our purpose and our goals reinforce each other, helping us navigate life with clarity, passion, and efficiency.

Long-Term Fulfillment

It is always tempting to chase after short-term rewards that bring momentary satisfaction but leave us feeling unfulfilled in the long run. Without a clear sense of purpose, we risk becoming stuck in a cycle of constantly seeking the next quick fix—a pattern that often leads to disappointment and a lingering sense of emptiness. A well-defined purpose statement changes this by anchoring us in something far deeper and more enduring.

Purpose offers us long-term fulfillment because it shifts our focus from short-lived pleasures to meaningful, impactful actions. Instead of chasing surface-level gratification, we find satisfaction in pursuits that align with our values, contribute to our personal growth, and positively impact the lives of others. Purpose helps us see beyond immediate distractions, reminding us of what truly matters, and inspiring us to invest our time and energy in ways that create lasting value.

When we are guided by purpose, our actions take on greater significance. Whether we're working toward a challenging goal, supporting those around us, or striving to grow into our best selves, purpose gives us a sense of direction and ensures that our efforts feel worthwhile. It transforms everyday tasks into opportunities to build something meaningful, helping us navigate life with clarity and intention.

By grounding us in a sense of meaning, purpose also creates a ripple effect that extends beyond ourselves. It inspires us to take actions that not only support our growth but also improve the well-being of others, whether that's within our families, communities, or the broader world. This eudaimonic approach to fulfillment offers a far deeper, more sustainable sense of happiness.

At its essence, our purpose statement helps us escape the distractions of the moment and focus on what truly matters in the long run. It ensures that our lives are guided by our values and intentions that lead to profound and lasting fulfillment, enabling us to thrive personally and in how we impact the world around us. Together, purpose and direction give us the tools to build a life of meaning, resilience, and enduring satisfaction.

CREATING YOUR PERSONAL PURPOSE STATEMENT

Now, let's take the first step toward operating at our peak performance by crafting our purpose statement. This isn't just a box to check—it's a deeply personal process that may take a few drafts to get it just right. You'll know you've nailed it when your purpose statement feels as essential to your daily life as your smartphone—something you not only want to have with you but truly can't imagine navigating life without. Let's begin.

Step 1. Identify Your Core Strengths

Since our purpose will naturally be rooted in our strengths, talents, and interests it's essential to confidently define those strengths. To assist in this process, we'll begin by taking the Virtues in Action (VIA) Survey of Character Strengths, a highly regarded and validated assessment generously available for free at www.authentichappiness.org under the Questionnaires tab. This assessment will help pinpoint the areas where we naturally excel, providing invaluable insights to build our purpose around these strengths. By doing so, we ensure our purpose is authentic and fosters sustained motivation, enabling us to thrive in ways that align with who we truly are. Do this now, and identify your top five strengths.

Step 2. Discover Your Passions and Motivations

Next, let's take a few minutes to reflect on our passions by asking ourselves some key questions that will guide us in introspectively evaluating what truly drives us:

- What activities do we genuinely enjoy participating in?
- What goals excite us and inspire energy for action?
- What talents do we possess that give us an advantage over others in the same field or activity?
- How can we use our strengths to make a positive impact on our family or community?
- What do we want to be remembered for?

By thoughtfully answering these questions, we gain a clearer understanding of how to harness our strengths and passions to make meaningful contributions to our environment. In doing so, we take intentional steps toward creating a lasting legacy, ensuring that the time we spend on this earth is impactful and aligned with our purpose.

Step 3. Establish Purpose-Driven Goals

We are now ready to create clear and measurable goals that bring our purpose to life. By breaking our purpose statement down into actionable long-term and short-term objectives, we ensure that our goals align with our core strengths and values. These goals should be thoughtfully crafted to provide balance in our lives, integrating both task engagement and the cultivation of strong, meaningful relationships. This approach creates a framework that fosters purpose, positive emotions, and meaningful achievements, allowing us to thrive personally and socially (often referred to as well-being) while remaining true to our purpose.

As an example, one of my goals is to:

Nurture my children by guiding them toward academic success, building their confidence, helping them achieve accredited credentials, and supporting them in pursuing fulfilling careers.

This goal represents one of four key areas that hold profound meaning in my life. Additionally, I have four specific sub-goals within this category (not shown here) that better align with the SMART goal format, ensuring I am clear as to what actions to take.

Step 4. Draft and Structure Your Purpose Statement

With steps one through three complete, we are now ready to write and refine our purpose statement. The format can be tailored to our personal preferences, but a helpful approach is to begin with a descriptive clause that highlights our top VIA character strengths. This introduction can then be followed by three to five declarative purpose statements outlining the areas where our energy and resources will be primarily directed.

We will complement each declarative statement with one to five SMART goals to make this actionable. These goals provide clear feedback and measurable milestones, helping us track progress and celebrate achievements along the way. My suggested format is outlined below:

PERSONAL PURPOSE STATEMENT

With *[virtue 1]*, *[virtue 2]*, and *[virtue 3]*, I commit to the following:

1. **Declarative Purpose Statement 1**
   a. Milestone 1
   b. Milestone 2
   c. Milestone 3
2. **Declarative Purpose Statement 2**
   a. Milestone 1
   b. Milestone 2
   c. Milestone 3
3. **Declarative Purpose Statement 3**
   a. Milestone 1
   b. Milestone 2
   c. Milestone 3

Step 5. Refine and Personalize Your Statement

This final step focuses on refining and perfecting your purpose statement. Begin by reading it carefully and examining its format. While it may already feel authentic and accurate, you will likely identify areas that can be adjusted to resonate more deeply with your true self. Take the time to make these adjustments and then re-evaluate your statement.

It is critical to avoid tailoring your purpose to fit social expectations or shaping it based on what you think others might find acceptable. Your purpose must be 100% authentic to what drives and inspires you. Remember, you will serve others most effectively when you are operating within your strengths and motivated by your genuine passion.

How will you know when your purpose statement is complete? You'll feel compelled to keep it close at all times—in your wallet, purse, Bible, computer bag, or briefcase. When your purpose statement transforms from a task to check off into a document that powerfully articulates your passionate purpose in life, you'll know you've found it. *It will no longer feel like just words on a page, but rather a reflection of who you are and what you are meant to achieve with the one life you've been given.*

CHAPTER 1 REFLECTION: HOW YOUR PURPOSE STATEMENT AFFECTS PEAK PERFORMANCE

Whether we cross the finish line of life filled with regret or overflowing with fulfillment and gratitude will largely depend on our discovery of and commitment to our purpose. While all 12 concepts explored in this book are essential to creating an extraordinary life, understanding and embracing our purpose is perhaps the most transformative.[4]

Effort without direction is like running in circles—it expends energy without meaningful results. Purpose provides the focus that transforms hard work into profound outcomes. It ensures that our efforts are aligned with what truly matters, allowing us to channel our talents, passions, and resources toward achieving something remarkable.

Without a clear purpose, even our most diligent work risks falling short of its potential. But when we operate within our purpose, we unlock the ability to excel as an outlier, achieving results that far surpass expectations and set us apart from our peers. Discovering and living with purpose is not just about success—it's about creating a life that is exceptional, impactful, and deeply fulfilling.

CHAPTER 1 ACTION ITEMS

- Complete the VIA strengths test. *(Time Commitment ~ 1 hour)*
- Complete your purpose statement rough draft. *(Time Commitment ~ 1 hour)*
- Create the final draft of your purpose statement. *(Time Commitment ~ 1 hour)*

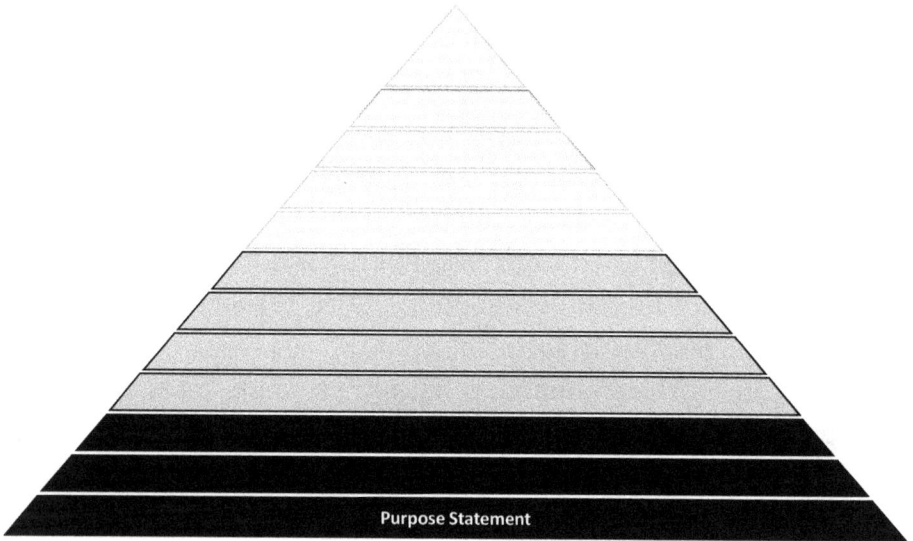

Purpose Statement

CHAPTER 2

POSITIVE PSYCHOLOGY
EMPOWERING PEAK PERFORMANCE THROUGH POSITIVITY

STORY: FINDING POSITIVITY DESPITE THE DARKNESS

Amidst one of history's darkest chapters, a man endured unthinkable suffering. Torn from his family, stripped of his possessions, and imprisoned in a Nazi concentration camp, he faced starvation, brutality, and the constant threat of death. Every shred of his identity and dignity was systematically stripped away—except for one thing: his ability to choose how he responded to his circumstances.

This man was Viktor Frankl, a psychiatrist whose extraordinary resilience and profound understanding of human psychology not only enabled him to survive the horrors of the Holocaust but also change the lives of millions. Frankl discovered that even in the most dehumanizing conditions, we can find meaning, hope, and purpose by focusing on what we can control—our mindset. He clung to positive visions of the future, memories of his wife's love, and a deep sense that his suffering could serve a greater purpose.

Frankl's unwavering positivity and commitment to surviving not only helped him endure the concentration camps but also inspired countless others around him. He often shared his insights on finding meaning in suffering with fellow prisoners, offering them hope and a sense of purpose amidst the despair. His ability to maintain a hopeful outlook and encourage others to do the same was a beacon of light in the darkest of times.

After surviving the war, Viktor Frankl shared his profound insights with the world, shaping the fields of psychology and psychiatry. He founded logotherapy, a groundbreaking approach that identifies the search for meaning as the central human motivation. His book, *Man's Search for Meaning*, became a timeless guide for overcoming hardship and living with purpose. Frankl's contributions earned him international recognition, including the Oskar Pfister Award from the American Psychiatric Association, professorships at esteemed institutions like Harvard and the University of Vienna, and numerous honorary doctorates. His legacy proves that even in the face of unimaginable adversity, a mindset of hope and purpose can fuel resilience and peak performance. In this chapter, we'll explore how to harness this principle of positivity as a protective factor for building a life of extraordinary achievement.

DEFINITION OF POSITIVE PSYCHOLOGY

Positive psychology marks a transformative shift in the field of psychological research, turning our focus from merely addressing psychological disorders and weaknesses to amplifying our strengths and virtues. Instead of just fixing what's wrong, it emphasizes enhancing our well-being, resilience, and physical health through intentional awareness, evidence-based interventions, and proactive behaviors. This strengths-based approach empowers us to take control of our circumstances and cultivate a life of flourishing and thriving.

At the heart of positive psychology lies the PERMA framework, pioneered by Dr. Martin Seligman and colleagues. PERMA identifies five dimensions essential to our well-being: Positive Emotion, Engagement, Relationships, Meaning, and Accomplishment. Each of these dimensions provides a distinct pathway for enhancing our life satisfaction—whether by fostering gratitude, finding joy in purposeful work, building meaningful connections, pursuing fulfilling goals, or celebrating achievements. What makes this framework especially impactful is that each pathway can be measured, developed, and strengthened independently.

Flourishing, a cornerstone of positive psychology, goes beyond simply being free of mental illness. It represents a state of optimal well-being characterized by positive emotions, engaging activities, fulfilling relationships, and a sense of meaningful accomplishment. With intentional effort and interventions focused on these PERMA dimensions, we can unlock our potential to flourish. Tools and exercises validated by research help us identify our strengths, uncover growth opportunities, and actively elevate our quality of life. [5,6]

Positive psychology invites us to reimagine what it means to live a thriving life. By aligning our strengths with a clear sense of purpose and committing to meaningful pursuits, we not only enhance our personal fulfillment but also contribute to the well-being of those around us. Taken together, we can design a life where thriving becomes the norm, not the exception.

THE IMPORTANCE OF POSITIVE PSYCHOLOGY FOR PEAK PERFORMANCE

A positive mindset is essential for peak performance because it shifts our focus from merely overcoming challenges to thriving by harnessing our strengths and aligning our actions with our purpose. We will be empowered to excel in all areas of life if we guard our positivity. When we foster positive emotions like gratitude, hope, and optimism, we build resilience and a stronger ability to bounce back from setbacks.

This resilience helps us stay fully engaged in our meaningful activities, putting our skills and passions to far better use. We also unlock focus, creativity, and flow where peak performance is unleashed. Additionally, we strengthen relationships providing us with support, collaboration, and a sense of belonging, which can significantly fuel our motivation and persistence. Pursuing a deeper sense of meaning in our work and personal lives inspires purpose-driven action. Finally, experiencing and celebrating accomplishments—no matter how small—reinforces confidence and sustains our momentum.[7,9]

For example, a student leveraging positive psychology might use gratitude practices to reduce stress during exams, while finding flow in focused study sessions to achieve academic excellence. Similarly, a professional aligning their work with personal values can find greater satisfaction, leading to skill improvement, competence, innovation, and career growth. In athletics, fostering optimism and strong team connections enhances individual performance, team camaraderie, and success.

By intentionally applying these principles, we don't just improve our well-being, we unlock a level of performance that allows us to flourish, achieve our goals, and make a meaningful impact on the community around us. Positive psychology is the science behind reaching new heights and thriving in every pursuit. Through the PERMA principles—Positive Emotion, Engagement, Relationships, Meaning, and Accomplishment— we gain valuable feedback that provides critical insights into our well-being while empowering us to achieve extraordinary results. Below is an expanded explanation of each element of Positive Psychology:

Positive Emotion

In positive psychology, positive emotion—ranging from joy, gratitude, and hope to serenity, pride, and inspiration—are more than moments of happiness but powerful drivers that influence how we think, act, and approach challenges. These emotions play a foundational role in enhancing our well-being and empowering us to perform at our best. They broaden our perspective and expand our cognitive abilities—a phenomenon psychologist Dr. Barbara Fredrickson calls the "broaden-and-build theory." When we experience positive emotions, our minds feel safe and become more open to creative problem-solving, learning, and connecting with others. This broadening effect enhances our ability to see possibilities and opportunities that might otherwise remain hidden, paving the way for innovative thinking and better decision-making—both critical for peak performance.[8]

Moreover, positive emotions help us build lasting psychological, social, and physical resources. For instance, feeling gratitude strengthens relationships and fosters collaboration. Experiencing hope motivates us to persist in the face of challenges, while pride in our accomplishments bolsters our self-efficacy and inspires us to aim higher. Over time, these cumulative benefits create a resilience reserve—a mental and emotional reservoir we can draw upon during periods of stress or adversity.[9, 10]

Positive emotions are also directly linked to our ability to enter and sustain a flow state, where we become fully immersed in our activity and perform at our highest level. When we cultivate joy or excitement about a task, we're more likely to stay engaged, overcome obstacles, and find fulfillment in the process. For example, an athlete who feels optimistic and inspired by their purpose is more likely to push through grueling training sessions, and a professional who feels passionate about their work is better equipped to tackle complex problems with enthusiasm while staying mentally attentive.[4]

Importantly, positive emotions are not about ignoring negative experiences or adopting a blind optimism. Instead, they involve cultivating an intentional awareness of the good moments, no matter how small, and leveraging them to fuel growth and resilience. Practices like gratitude journaling, savoring achievements, and mindfulness exercises help amplify these emotions, creating a ripple effect that uplifts our overall performance.[6, 9]

Engagement

Engagement, in the PERMA framework, represents a state of deep involvement where we are fully absorbed in what we are doing. This type of engagement is more than simply being busy—it's about connecting with activities that challenge us, resonate with our values, and make use of our unique strengths and purpose. In positive psychology, engagement is closely tied to the concept of *flow*, a term coined by Mihaly Csikszentmihalyi to describe a state of complete immersion in a task. When we are in flow, everything else fades away. We experience intense focus and an effective rhythm as challenges and skills align perfectly.

This kind of engagement is essential for peak performance. It allows us to tap into intrinsic motivation—the drive that comes from within—by making the process itself rewarding, not just the outcome. When deeply engaged, we are more resilient, as challenges feel less overwhelming since we are focused on the task rather than its potential difficulties. Engagement also accelerates mastery; the focused attention we give to a meaning-ful pursuit enables us to learn and grow much faster. Whether it's a surgeon performing a delicate operation, an athlete in the middle of a high-stakes game, or a musician immersed in a beautiful performance, engagement is often the key to peak performance and extraordinary achievement.

Cultivating engagement in our own lives requires inten-tional effort. Aligning tasks with our strengths can make activ-ities feel more natural and enjoyable. Creating an environment that minimizes distractions allows us to stay focused and present. When we set clear goals and pursue challenges that stretch us just enough to stay exciting but not overwhelming, we create the conditions for flow to exist. Mental attentiveness also plays a role in engagement, helping us stay in the moment and immerse ourselves fully in the activity at hand.

Engagement doesn't just elevate individual performance; it inspires those around us. A teacher deeply involved in their lesson can spark curiosity and focus in their students, while a leader passionate about their mission can energize a team to achieve remarkable results. The ripple effect of engagement extends to families, communities, and organizations, creating a culture of purpose and achievement.

Ultimately, engagement is the bridge between effort and excellence, the connection between striving and thriving. It is how we find fulfillment not just in what we accomplish but in the process of our work itself. When we embrace engagement, we open the door to peak performance, a life of deeper mean-ing with our tasks.

Relationships

Relationships, in the PERMA framework, are founda-tional to both our well-being and our ability to achieve

peak performance. Positive psychology emphasizes the importance of meaningful connections with others, as strong relationships provide support, encouragement, and a sense of
belonging. These bonds are not merely a source of comfort—
they are also a key driver of success. When we cultivate
healthy relationships, we create an environment that fosters collaboration, trust, and mutual respect. This not only
enhances our resilience in the face of challenges but also provides the psychological safety needed to take risks, learn from
failure, and grow.

From a performance perspective, relationships can be
transformative. Mentors guide us, teammates push us to
excel, and loved ones provide the motivation to persist when
the road gets tough. Research consistently shows that people
who feel supported by others are more likely to achieve their
goals and maintain their focus under pressure. Furthermore,
the act of supporting others boosts our own sense of purpose
and fulfillment, creating a cycle of positivity that drives higher
levels of engagement and achievement.[10]

Incorporating relationships into our pursuit of peak performance requires deliberate and intentional effort. By building
trust, practicing empathy, and showing genuine appreciation,
we strengthen our connections and create a foundation for
mutual support. Simple acts like active listening or expressing
gratitude can deepen these bonds, fostering an environment of
understanding and care. One powerful tool in this process is
Active Constructive Responding (ACR), where we celebrate the
successes of those we care about with enthusiasm and support,
reinforcing the value of our relationships. When we invest in
meaningful connections, we not only enrich our own lives but
also unlock the collective strength of collaboration, inspiration,
and shared success. Ultimately, relationships are a cornerstone

of well-being—they are an important aspect behind achieving meaningful outcomes in our lives.[11]

Meaningful Goals

Meaningful goals, in the PERMA framework, emphasize the importance of pursuing goals that resonate with our values and purpose, as these provide a deep sense of fulfillment and direction. Unlike temporary or superficial objectives that frequently pop up in our lives, meaningful goals inspire intrinsic motivation, creating a powerful drive that sustains us through challenges and setbacks. When our goals align with our sense of identity and long-term aspirations, they not only fuel our growth but also enhance our overall sense of purpose and well-being.

From a performance perspective, meaningful goals act as a compass, guiding our actions and keeping us focused on what truly matters. They foster clarity, helping us prioritize our efforts and make decisions that are congruent with our values. Research shows that people who set meaningful goals experience greater engagement, resilience, and satisfaction as they work toward them. Moreover, achieving these goals provides a sense of accomplishment, reinforcing our confidence in our abilities and motivating us to endure the long game.[12]

Incorporating meaningful goals into our pursuit of peak performance calls for thoughtful reflection and intentional planning. It begins with identifying what truly matters to us, then breaking down long-term ambitions into actionable, manageable steps. Celebrating progress along the way reinforces our commitment and keeps us energized for the journey ahead. By aligning our daily actions with a greater purpose, we unlock the motivation and resilience needed to excel. Ultimately, meaningful goals transform distant ambitions into achievable milestones, reminding us that even the loftiest aspirations are conquered one deliberate step at a time.

Achievement

Achievement, in the PERMA framework, emphasizes the importance of setting and accomplishing goals that challenge us, providing a sense of purpose and fulfillment. Achievements are not simply outcomes; they represent milestones in our personal growth and evidence of our ability to overcome obstacles and get tasks out the door. Whether big or small, each accomplishment builds our confidence, enhances our resilience, and motivates us to strive toward another success.

From a performance perspective, achievement provides fuel and inertia to pursue our purpose. Reaching a goal reinforces our belief in our capabilities, while the process itself—marked by effort, learning, and adaptation—develops critical skills that further elevate our performance while preparing us for future tasks. Research demonstrates that a consistent focus on achievement fosters a growth mindset, encouraging us to see challenges as opportunities for improvement rather than threats to our abilities. This mindset not only helps us succeed in the short term but also lays the foundation for long-term excellence.[13]

Incorporating achievement into our pursuit of peak performance requires clarity, commitment, and deliberate action. Defining meaningful goals, breaking them into manageable steps, and celebrating progress along the way are essential practices. Each success, no matter how small, contributes to a positive feedback loop that strengthens our resolve and keeps us focused on what matters most. Ultimately, achievement provides us the needed dopamine and energy to know our efforts are producing results.

Enhancing Positivity in Your Life

Positivity is not a single emotion, rather, it's a transformative practice that leads to a richer, more meaningful life. While life's circumstances may rise and fall, positivity allows us to navigate these changes with hope and resilience. The key lies in intentionality: by making deliberate choices aligned with the PERMA framework, we can cultivate lasting well-being. These five elements—Positive Emotion, Engagement, Relationships, Meaning, and Accomplishment—serve as measurable markers, helping us to cultivate lives of greater joy, connection, and fulfillment.

By focusing on these small, actionable steps to strengthen each PERMA element, we can elevate not only how we feel but also how we function across all areas of life. While this is a journey that requires patience and persistence, the alternative is pessimism, helplessness, and hopelessness, which strangle the life out of so many. Remember, enhancing positivity is not about overnight transformation—it's about gradual improvements in our well-being.

It's important to recognize that our capacity for positivity is influenced by our experiences, environment, and current mindset. While these factors shape our outlook, they do not define our potential for change. The greatest barrier to cultivating positivity is hopelessness—the belief that our future will not be better than our present regardless of our efforts. When we lose hope, we stop striving for change and settle for the status quo.

To combat this, embrace every small improvement as a victory. Celebrate progress, no matter how modest it may seem. If the idea of tackling all five PERMA elements feels overwhelming, focus on just one—perhaps the area that feels most pressing, such as nurturing relationships or finding deeper engagement in daily tasks. Each step forward, however small, lays the foundation for a brighter future.

By committing to this practice of improvement and allowing yourself grace along the way, you are not only enhancing positivity—you are creating a life filled with hope and growth. Let PERMA be a journey you embark on with optimism and confidence, knowing that even the smallest effort can lead to exciting change.

Step 1. Cultivate Positive Emotions

The foundation of positivity lies in fostering positive emotions. To begin, assess your current state of well-being using the PERMA Meter questionnaire, available for free at www.authentichappiness.org. This evidence-based tool, located in the flourishing questionnaires section, offers valuable insights into your strengths and areas for growth across the five dimensions of Positive Psychology (PERMA). By identifying where you are now, you can better chart your path toward flourishing.[14]

To enhance positive emotions, focus on intentional practices like gratitude, mindfulness, and savoring. For example, keeping a brief gratitude journal allows you to reflect on the good in your life, shifting attention from challenges to blessings. Daily mindfulness routines, such as spending designated time encouraging your family or spending a few minutes fully immersed in nature, can help ground you in the present moment. Savoring life's joys—whether it's relishing a delicious meal, pausing to admire a sunset, or celebrating small victories—strengthens your ability to experience positive emotions more deeply and for longer durations. These practices not only improve how you feel now but also equip you to better navigate future challenges.

Positive Psychology emphasizes that cultivating positivity is not merely about chasing pleasure or avoiding discomfort.

While pleasure offers immediate, narrow-focused rewards, positive emotions broaden our attention, helping us recognize opportunities and prepare for future tasks. This distinction is critical: thriving often requires embracing the full spectrum of experiences, including the negative, as they can motivate us toward meaningful growth. For instance, challenges like loss or failure may initially trigger negative emotions, but they also provide opportunities for resilience, purpose, and connection when approached with a growth mindset.[15]

Finally, remember that cultivating positive emotions is a skill—one that can be learned and strengthened over time. Begin by identifying what genuinely makes you feel good, whether it's spending time with loved ones, pursuing goal-congruent growth, exercising, or simply enjoying quiet moments of reflection. Incorporate these activities into your routine and celebrate the progress you make. By learning to hope for the best, embrace the upside, and seize opportunities, you create a foundation for long-term well-being and success. Positive emotions are not just an end in themselves; they are the important fuel that keeps us moving toward becoming our best selves.

Step 2. Increase Task Engagement

Engagement flourishes when we immerse ourselves in activities that align with our skills, passions, and values. This deep focus can bring us into a flow state where we are fully absorbed in the moment. To achieve this, we should seek tasks that challenge us just enough to sharpen our focus without causing overwhelming stress. These meaningful challenges keep us energized and engaged, providing the right balance of effort and reward. Whether it's solving a complex problem as a student, pursuing a creative project as a musician, or tackling an assigned task at work, these activities push our potential and help us thrive.[9]

The VIA Survey of Character Strengths is, again, a vital tool for connecting our efforts with our personal strengths, as it helps identify the unique traits that bring out our best. These strengths, which were used to shape our purpose statement in Chapter 1, should guide our daily activities and remain at the forefront of our minds. Regularly revisiting them and intentionally weaving them into our tasks ensures that we remain aligned with our authentic selves. For example, someone whose top strength is creativity might find immense satisfaction in brainstorming innovative solutions at work or exploring artistic hobbies. Their strength not only keeps them engaged but also allows them to persist where others would give up, turning challenges into opportunities for growth. Our peak performance will not come from our weaknesses.

By aligning our daily efforts with our character strengths and passions, we unlock extraordinary levels of energy, focus, and fulfillment. This intentional alignment transforms routine tasks into meaningful endeavors, fueling both positivity and peak performance. Imagine waking up every day excited to tackle challenges because they resonate deeply with who you are and what you stand for. The result is a life that feels purposeful, and driven by activities that bring out the best in us. Engagement isn't just about productivity—it's about finding joy and flow in what we do, empowering us to achieve our highest potential while staying connected to our core values.

Step 3. Strengthening Relationships

Strong relationships are vital for positivity and peak performance, and improving them often starts with communication. One powerful strategy is Active Constructive

Responding (ACR) mentioned at the beginning of this chapter. This method of celebrating others' successes in a way that deepens bonds. When someone shares good news, respond with enthusiasm and genuine interest. For example, instead of a simple "That's nice," an ACR response would include asking questions, expressing excitement, and encouraging the person to share more details. You can also ask questions about their experience while expressing excitement for their achievement. This approach builds trust, fosters mutual support, and strengthens your emotional connections. By being intentional about how you engage with others, you create a foundation of positivity that uplifts everyone involved.

Step 4. Finding Meaning in Your Daily Life

Incorporating meaningful actions into your daily life becomes much more intentional when you regularly revisit the personal purpose statement you've already crafted. This statement serves as your guiding light, helping you make choices that align with your core values while steering you away from tasks that feel empty or unfulfilling. It empowers you to say "no" to pseudo-work and to evaluate your efforts with clarity, ensuring that your time and energy are spent on what truly matters. For example, if your purpose centers around creativity and connection, you might prioritize collaborative projects that spark innovation, while finding ways to streamline or delegate repetitive, low-value tasks that don't contribute to your greater mission.

When your daily activities reflect your purpose, even routine or challenging tasks can feel rewarding. The process of alignment between purpose and action not only reduces the frustration of "busy work" but also enhances your sense of accomplishment. Imagine how much more satisfying your day becomes when your tasks resonate with your values. It is far more rewarding when your work feels like a step toward something greater, rather than a series of disconnected obligations. By consciously aligning your efforts with your purpose, you create a sense of direction and fulfillment that keeps you motivated and focused.

Over time, this alignment builds momentum. Each action taken with intention reinforces your commitment to your goals and your belief in their significance. The result is a virtuous cycle where meaningful work drives personal growth and satisfaction, energizing you to tackle even greater challenges. Revisiting your purpose statement regularly ensures that your actions stay on track, allowing you to adapt and grow as your vision evolves. This intentional approach transforms daily effort into meaningful progress, fueling both positivity and peak performance.

Step 5. Celebrate Accomplishments

Accomplishment is not merely about crossing the finish line. You must also recognize and appreciate the journey that brings you closer to your goals. Each step forward, no matter how small, is a building block toward peak performance. For instance, an athlete training for a marathon doesn't just celebrate race day; they find satisfaction in hitting a new personal best during practice or completing a challenging workout. Fueling our motivation requires recognizing incremental progress, which allows us to cultivate a sense of achievement and keep moving forward. This perspective helps us appreciate the process, which is where the real growth occurs.

One of the most effective ways to foster this sense of accomplishment is to set meaningful goals and break them into manageable steps. Large ambitions can feel overwhelming, but dividing them into smaller milestones makes them feel achievable and keeps us motivated. For example, a professional aiming for a promotion might set intermediate goals like learning a new skill, completing a major project, or receiving positive feedback from peers. Celebrating each of these milestones—whether with a moment of personal reflection, a reward, or sharing success with a mentor—reinforces the belief that progress is possible and worthwhile. These small wins act as stepping stones that build momentum toward the larger goal.

Tracking progress is another powerful strategy to enhance your sense of accomplishment and maintain focus. Tools like journals, habit trackers, or apps can help document daily efforts and measure how far you've come. This not only provides tangible proof of your hard work but also boosts motivation by showcasing the cumulative results of consistent effort. For example, a student preparing for a major exam might schedule specific study sessions and review their progress weekly, creating a visual reminder of their dedication and improvement. Reflecting on these achievements encourages a mastery mindset, where challenges are viewed as opportunities to improve rather than obstacles to fear. By regularly acknowledging and celebrating your accomplishments, you lay the foundation for sustained motivation and peak performance regardless of the length of the journey.

CHAPTER 2 REFLECTION: HOW YOUR POSITIVITY AFFECTS YOUR PEAK PERFORMANCE

Enhancing positivity is an intentional process that transforms how we experience life, providing the emotional fuel necessary for peak performance. The PERMA framework of Positive Emotion, Engagement, Relationships, Meaning, and Accomplishment empowers us to rise above challenges, broaden our perspectives, and seize opportunities for growth. Each element of PERMA contributes uniquely to our well-being: Positive Emotion fuels our creativity and motivation, Engagement immerses us in meaningful pursuits, Relationships provide support and connection, Meaning infuses our actions with purpose, and Accomplishment builds confidence through achievement. Together, these elements form the foundation of a thriving and fulfilling life.

Positivity is not a passive state—it requires deliberate effort and consistent practice. By consciously choosing to focus on gratitude, mindfulness, and the joys of daily life, we can train our minds to notice opportunities rather than obstacles. For example, savoring moments of success or connection allows us to internalize their significance, fueling resilience and perseverance.

Positivity doesn't erase life's difficulties but equips us to face them with courage and optimism. In this way, positivity becomes a dynamic force, helping us to adapt, overcome setbacks, and unlock our full potential in both personal and professional endeavors. By intentionally fostering these emotions in our daily lives, we not only enhance our happiness and well-being but also unlock new levels of understanding, ability, and resilience—setting the stage for a truly extraordinary life.

Chapter 2 Action Items

- Assess your current well-being using the PERMA Meter questionnaire. *(Time Commitment ~ 30 minutes)*
- Identify areas of PERMA to cultivate and make a plan. *(Time Commitment ~ 1 hour)*

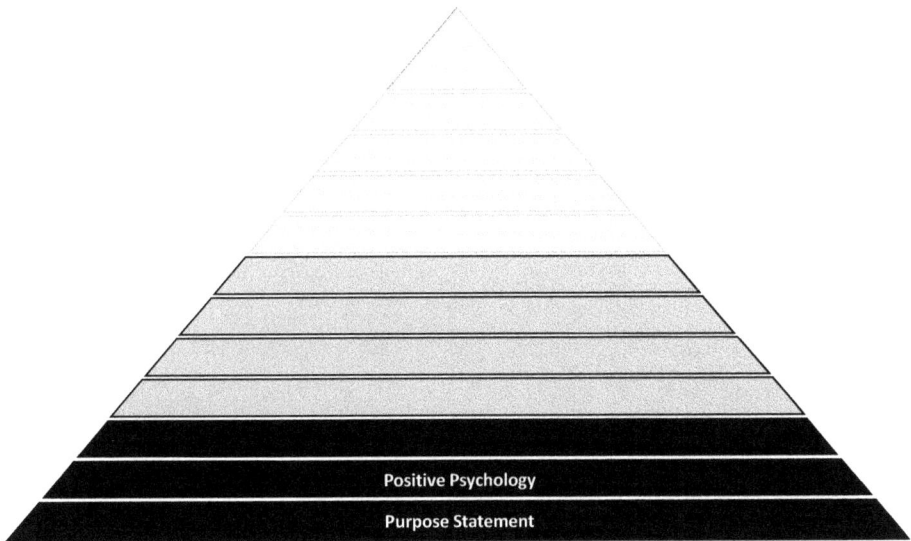

Positive Psychology

Purpose Statement

CHAPTER 3

GOAL ORIENTATION
CULTIVATING A MASTERY MINDSET

STORY: THE POWER OF THE MASTERY MINDSET

At just 13 years old, Olympic swimmer Katie Ledecky set her sights on something greater than medals—she pursued mastery. While many athletes focused solely on beating their rivals, Ledecky fixated on refining her stroke, improving her endurance, and pushing her personal limits. Rather than measuring success by the podium, she measured it by progress. Her relentless commitment to mastery, rather than mere performance, led her to shatter world records and dominate the sport for over a decade. However, her path to becoming one of the greatest swimmers in history was not without obstacles.

In 2012, at just 15 years old, Ledecky shocked the world by winning Olympic gold in the 800-meter freestyle—an event in which she wasn't expected to win medal. While many might have been content with reaching the pinnacle of their sport so early, she used that victory as fuel to keep improving. She didn't just want to win; she wanted to redefine what was possible in distance swimming. Over the next decade, she relentlessly pursued perfection in her training, often swimming upwards of 8,000 meters per session, fine-tuning her technique, and pushing through grueling workouts designed to test her limits. Despite her dominance, she also faced setbacks. At the 2020 Tokyo Olympics, she lost two races to rising competitors, marking the first time she had been truly challenged on the Olympic stage. Instead of letting those defeats define her, she refocused on her process, doubling down on the mastery mindset that had brought her success.

Ledecky's unwavering dedication paid off. She has won a staggering nine Olympic gold medals, four silver medals, and one bronze medal, making her one of the most decorated female swimmers of all time. She has also claimed 21 World Championship titles—the most of any female swimmer in history—and set 16 world records over the course of her career. But what makes her truly exceptional isn't just the records or the medals—it's her mindset. She continues to chase improvement, never settling for past success, always refining, always growing.

Ledecky's story exemplifies the transformative power of the mastery goal orientation. Those who chase external validation often burn out, but those who focus on continuous growth unlock an endless well of motivation. By choosing a mastery approach, you shift from possible, yet temporary, success to sustainable excellence, ensuring that each step forward fuels the next. In this chapter, we'll explore how shaping your goal orientation with intention and focus can empower you to achieve extraordinary results—not just in competition, but in every aspect of life.

DEFINITION OF A GOAL ORIENTATION

Goal orientation refers to the mindset we adopt when pursuing our goals, shaping how we respond to stress and obstacles that inevitably arise along the way. Research has identified four primary orientations: mastery approach, performance approach, mastery avoidance, and performance avoidance. Among these, the mastery approach is consistently shown to be the most effective at producing long-term results. Individuals with this orientation focus on continuous improvement, prioritizing learning and long-term development rather than measuring success by comparison to others. This mindset fosters resilience, intrinsic motivation, and a deep engagement with personal growth.[16, 17]

In contrast, a performance approach orientation centers on proving one's ability, with success defined by outperforming others and gaining external validation. While this approach can sometimes yield short-term gains, it carries significant risks when prioritized as the dominant mindset—both for individuals and organizations. Over time, a fixation on performance outcomes can lead to avoidance behaviors, deception, blind spots, anxiety, and even ethical compromises, as individuals become more concerned with appearing successful than with actual growth and skill improvement.[18]

The two avoidance-oriented mindsets—mastery avoidance and performance avoidance—stem from a focus on avoiding failure rather than improvement. Mastery avoidance occurs when individuals are primarily driven by a desire to meet minimum standards or avoid falling short of their past achievements. This orientation can limit ambition, leading to stagnation rather than progress. Performance avoidance, on the other hand, is rooted in a deep fear of failure, causing individuals to shy away from challenges where they might appear incompetent. This mindset stifles innovation, risk-taking, and long-term success. Ultimately, understanding these orientations allows us to intentionally cultivate a mastery approach, enabling peak performance, sustained growth, and a mindset that thrives in the face of adversity.

Which orientation we adopt in a given situation—or as our dominant default approach in general—depends on a blend of our goal structure, past experiences, and beliefs about our intelligence. If our environment (goal structure) prioritizes effort and progress (such as a coach or teacher valuing improvement over results), we are more likely to develop a mastery-oriented mindset. However, if we are frequently judged or punished based on rankings or outcomes, a performance-based orientation may take hold.

Our past experiences with success and failure also play a crucial role. Someone who has been rewarded for effort and resilience may lean toward mastery goals, while those who have faced harsh criticism for mistakes might gravitate toward avoidance. Additionally, our beliefs about our intelligence—whether we see ability as fixed or malleable—strongly influence our orientation. If we believe skills can be developed with effort, we are more likely to embrace challenges and adopt a mastery approach. If we see intelligence as fixed, we may prioritize proving our competence (performance approach) or avoiding situations where our ego may be at risk (performance avoidance).

Understanding our goal orientation is critical to achieving peak performance because it dictates how we handle obstacles, growth, and motivation. While performance-based mindsets may often be the norm and can sometimes lead to short-term success, they usually result in burnout or anxiety ultimately resulting in more trouble than progress. A mastery approach, on the other hand, fuels long-term excellence by fostering resilience, intrinsic motivation, and a love for improvement. By recognizing the factors that shape our goal orientation, we can intentionally cultivate a mindset that pushes us toward continuous improvement and extraordinary achievement.

The Importance of Goal Orientation for Peak Performance

The way we approach our goals profoundly impacts our ability to achieve peak performance. A mastery-oriented mindset —where the focus is on growth, learning, and long-term development—allows individuals and organizations to embrace challenges, adapt to setbacks, and innovate at the highest level. In contrast, a performance-driven mindset, particularly when it leans toward proving ability rather than improving ability, can create serious roadblocks to sustained excellence. While a performance approach may sound great while yielding short-term wins, it usually does so at the cost of long-term success, ethical decision-making, and overall resilience.

One of the greatest risks of a performance approach is its tendency to increase anxiety and discourage risk-taking—especially when performance is under constant evaluation. When individuals are primarily focused on external validation rather than internal growth, they begin to avoid challenges where success is uncertain, put down team members, silo resources and knowledge, and lose motivation when rewards or recognition are absent. This narrow focus on immediate performance outcomes prioritizes short-term gains over long-term mastery. This can even lead to a culture where deception is rewarded over innovation. For example, in high-stakes environments where failure is punished, employees may choose to hide problems rather than address them, fearing that exposing challenges could damage their reputation. This fear-driven avoidance ultimately stifles learning and growth, preventing breakthroughs that could lead to sustained success.

A real-world case of this destructive performance orientation can be seen in the Volkswagen emissions scandal.
Engineers and executives, operating under intense pressure
to outperform competitors in sales, chose to manipulate
emissions data rather than solve the underlying engineering
challenges. Their performance-avoidance culture discouraged
learning and innovation, creating a corporate-wide cover-up
rather than genuine technological progress. Had Volkswagen
embraced a mastery approach, engineers would have been
encouraged to tackle setbacks head-on, take calculated risks,
and persist through difficulties to develop or, at least, improve
legitimate low-emission technology. Instead, the short-term
fixation on performance led to financial and reputational
disaster. This highlights why cultivating a mastery mindset is
critical—not just for individual success, but for organizational
integrity, long-term innovation, and industry leadership.
True peak performance is achieved not by cutting corners,
but by embracing hard work, learning from failure, and
continuously striving for excellence. Those who prioritize
mastery over performance will ultimately outperform those
who chase only immediate success.[19]

Building on the importance of goal orientation, it is crucial to understand the four primary orientations and how
they shape our performance, decision-making, and long-term
success. These orientations determine how we respond to
stress, setbacks, and opportunities for growth. By recognizing
the strengths and limitations of each, we can consciously and
purposefully shape our mindset to achieve peak performance.

Performance Avoidance is the least adaptive of all orientations.
This orientation is rooted in the fear of failure and the desire
to avoid looking incompetent. Individuals with this mindset

often withdraw from challenges, choosing safety over prog-ress to minimize the risk of embarrassment. This avoidance stifles growth, as it prevents people from taking necessary risks, seeking feedback, or pushing beyond their comfort zones. In high-stakes environments, performance avoidance can lead to paralysis, dishonesty, accidents, and missed opportunities, as people become more focused on not failing than on actually succeeding. Over time, this orientation breeds low confidence, stagnation, and, at best, mediocrity.

Mastery Avoidance, while less detrimental than performance avoidance, still presents significant challenges. Those with this mindset are primarily motivated by the fear of failing to meet either an organizational benchmark or their own inter-nal standards, often leading them to set rigid or unrealis-tic expectations. Instead of striving for excellence, they may become preoccupied with doing just enough to avoid falling short, prioritizing consistency over true progress. Some obsess over perfection, fearing any deviation from their established competence, while others simply aim to meet minimum require-ments to avoid scrutiny or criticism. This defensive approach to mastery creates a rigid and unforgiving attitude toward growth, where avoiding mistakes becomes more important than pursuing meaningful skill development. As a result, mas-tery avoidance discourages risk-taking, experimentation, and bold problem-solving—ultimately stagnating innovation and limiting the pursuit of peak performance.

Performance Approach orientation shifts the focus toward demonstrating ability and outperforming others, which can be both motivating and risky. This mindset can drive indi-viduals to push themselves harder, chase external validation, and strive for competitive success, sometimes leading to high achievement in the short term. However, when the emphasis is purely on results rather than progress, individuals may take shortcuts, avoid difficult tasks where success isn't guaranteed, or sacrifice long-term development for immediate recognition. In organizations, a strong performance approach culture can foster unethical decision-making, deception, and anxiety, as seen in the Volkswagen scandal.

Another major drawback of a performance approach orientation emerges when individuals experience failure or defeat. Since their self-worth is often tied to winning, setbacks can lead to self-doubt, performance anxiety, and disengagement. Athletes, students, and professionals who rely on outperforming others for confidence may react to losses with anger, frustration, and even poor sportsmanship, struggling to cope when they fall short. In extreme cases, the fear of failure can push individuals toward performance-enhancing drugs, dishonest tactics, or quitting altogether, rather than using setbacks as opportunities for growth. While competition and external benchmarks can provide valuable motivation, relying too heavily on them creates a fragile system dependent on constant validation rather than intrinsic development.

Mastery Approach orientation is the most adaptive of all goal orientations, as it prioritizes growth, learning, and long-term development over immediate results or external validation. Those with this mindset embrace challenges, view setbacks as opportunities for improvement, and focus on personal progress rather than comparison to others. This orientation fosters resilience, intrinsic motivation, teamwork, and a deeper engagement with tasks, leading to sustainable success over time. Unlike performance-oriented individuals who may fear failure, those with a mastery approach recognize failure as a natural and valuable part of the learning process, allowing them to refine their skills and push beyond their previous limits.

However, a mastery approach is not without its challenges. Without clear, time-bound goals, individuals may become complacent in their efforts, endlessly pursuing improvement without a sense of urgency. When failure lacks immediate consequences, it may not create the pressure needed to drive meaningful progress. Effective mastery-oriented individuals must strike a balance—embracing growth while also setting concrete deadlines and benchmarks that prevent stagnation. Furthermore, maintaining a mastery approach can be especially difficult in environments that prioritize short-term performance outcomes. When working alongside those with a performance approach, individuals focused on long-term mastery may initially appear to be falling behind, as performance-driven peers achieve quick but often unsustainable results.

In these moments, it can be tempting to abandon mastery in favor of chasing external validation. However, the true power of a mastery approach lies in its ability to create enduring success, even if it doesn't always deliver immediate victories. Those who stay committed to growth, despite setbacks or external pressures, ultimately outperform their performance-driven counterparts over time. By combining the persistence of mastery with strategic goal-setting, individuals can ensure they don't just improve—but do so efficiently, effectively, and with lasting impact.

EMBRACING MASTERY APPROACH IN YOUR LIFE

Developing a mastery approach to goal orientation is not something that happens by chance—it requires intentional effort and a mindset shift toward long-term growth. While external pressures often push us toward performance-based thinking, we can take specific steps to cultivate an internal drive that prioritizes learning, resilience, and progress over quick results. By making deliberate changes in how we set goals, handle setbacks, and measure success, we create an environment where peak performance thrives. The following steps will help you embrace and strengthen a mastery approach orientation in your life:

Step 1. Set Development-Based Goals

Shift your focus from outcome-driven goals to learning-based ones. Instead of aiming to "win" or "be the best," set goals that prioritize progress, skill development, and deep understanding. When goals are centered solely on results—such as winning a race, landing a promotion, or getting a perfect score—the journey becomes rigid and anxiety-inducing. Success is then defined only by external validation, leaving little room for adaptability and growth. A development-based goal, on the other hand, focuses on improving abilities, refining techniques, and gaining deeper knowledge. For example, rather than striving to "get a promotion," focus on "mastering leadership communication" or "becoming an expert in my field." By committing to the process of learning, you shift from a mindset of pressure and fear of failure to one that embraces flexibility and continuous improvement.

Consider the difference in mindset when approaching a college course. A performance-driven student might focus entirely on getting an A, often resorting to memorization, cramming, or doing the bare minimum required to secure a high grade. While this might yield short-term results, the knowledge is often shallow and quickly forgotten. A mastery-oriented student, however, approaches the class with the goal of truly understanding the material and being able to apply it effectively. They engage deeply in discussions, seek connections between concepts, and actively use the knowledge beyond just exams. Ironically, by prioritizing learning over grades, they often achieve higher scores naturally—because they have internalized the material rather than simply performing for assessments. This shift in focus ensures lasting expertise and a foundation for future success, rather than temporary achievement.

Step 2. Adopt a Growth Mindset

Your beliefs about intelligence and ability directly shape your goal orientation. If you view intelligence as fixed—something you either have or don't—you will likely default to a performance-oriented mindset, avoiding challenges that could expose your limitations. However, if you adopt a growth mindset, you recognize that intelligence and skills are not set in stone but developed through effort, persistence, and learning. This shift in perspective transforms challenges from threats into opportunities, making setbacks a natural and valuable part of the learning process rather than a sign of inadequacy.

One of the most powerful ways to reinforce a growth mindset is to embrace an iterative theory of intelligence, where skills are developed through continuous refinement rather than innate talent. Imagine someone learning to play the piano. A person with a fixed mindset might assume that musical ability is something you must be born with, leading them to give up if progress is slow. In contrast, someone with a growth mindset understands that mastery comes through repetition, feedback, and small, consistent improvements. They embrace mistakes as part of the process, analyze what went wrong, and adjust their approach with each practice session. Over time, they build not only their technical skill but also the confidence that comes from knowing they can grow through effort.

To strengthen your growth mindset, intentionally expose yourself to environments that reinforce this perspective. Surround yourself with mentors who emphasize learning over innate talent, read books that highlight stories of persistence (especially in your field of interest), and seek out challenges that push you beyond your comfort zone. When you encounter difficulties, remind yourself that struggle is an essential part of mastery—every expert was once a beginner, and every break-through was preceded by setbacks. By shifting your focus from proving your ability to improving it, you set yourself up for sustained success and peak performance.

Step 3. Measure Success by Progress, Not Comparison

A mastery approach thrives on self-improvement rather than external validation. When your primary focus is on outper-forming others, success becomes unstable—you may feel confi-dent when you are ahead but discouraged the moment someone surpasses you. Instead of measuring yourself against others, shift your focus inward and track your personal growth over time. By prioritizing progress over comparison, you maintain motivation and ensure that your achievements are grounded in real skill development.

One of the most effective ways to do this is by setting mea-surable milestones in your skill development and regularly tracking your progress. For example, rather than comparing your running speed to someone else's, track how much your own pace has improved over the past month. If you're learning a new language, focus on how many new words or phrases you can use compared to last week, rather than how fluent someone else seems. Consider a student in a difficult course—if they fixate on scoring higher than their classmates, they may become discouraged when they don't immediately excel. However, if they track their progress based on how well they understand and apply the material, they'll stay motivated by their own improvement, letting the grades come naturally as a reflection of their mastery.

By regularly reflecting on your progress, you also create opportunities for necessary course corrections. If you hit a plateau or struggle with a particular concept, you can identify the issue early and adjust your approach—whether by seeking guidance, refining your strategy, or putting in additional practice. Tracking progress not only reinforces motivation but also provides clarity on when to push forward, when to pivot, and when to seek help. The more you embrace this mindset, the more sustainable and fulfilling your pursuit of excellence will become.

Step 4. Reframe Failure as a Learning Tool

One of the greatest advantages of the mastery approach is its ability to neutralize the fear of failure. Instead of seeing failure as a reflection of your abilities, reframe it as a stepping stone toward improvement. Every setback provides valuable feedback, exposing gaps in your knowledge, weaknesses in your strategy, or areas that need refinement. When something doesn't go as planned, resist the urge to dwell on disappointment. Instead, treat the experience like an experiment—analyze what went wrong, adjust your approach, and move forward with an improved process. Failure only becomes a stopping point if you let it.

Consider an athlete training for a marathon who falls short of their goal time in a qualifying race. If they view this as proof that they aren't capable, they may lose motivation or even quit. However, if they adopt a mastery approach, they'll analyze the race: Did they start too fast? Were they lacking endurance in the final miles? Was their fueling strategy ineffective? By identifying the specific reason for their struggle, they can adjust their training, refine their pacing, and return stronger for the next race. Similarly, a student who fails a difficult exam can either assume they "just aren't good at the subject" or recognize that their study method wasn't effective. If they assess where they went wrong—whether it was poor time management, surface-level memorization, or misunderstanding key concepts—they can adapt their approach, seek help, and improve on the next test.

By embracing failure as part of the learning process, you remove unnecessary pressure and unlock greater resilience. The most successful people in any field—from elite athletes to world-class scientists—have all experienced failure, but they didn't let it define them. Instead, they treated it as information, adjusted their approach, and kept progressing. The mastery approach allows you to do the same, turning obstacles into opportunities for growth.

Step 5. Push Beyond Your Comfort Zone

A mastery approach blooms when we continually push our boundaries, embracing challenges that stretch our abilities. Instead of avoiding difficult tasks where success isn't guaranteed, actively seek out situations that require you to grow—whether it's tackling a complex project, learning an entirely new skill, or competing against stronger opponents. These experiences accelerate improvement and prevent stagnation. The key is to lean into discomfort, understanding that struggle is not a sign of inadequacy but rather an indicator of progress. True mastery doesn't come from staying where you're already proficient; it comes from deliberately testing and expanding your limits.

Stepping outside of your comfort zone requires patience and the ability to resist the lure of short-term validation. In many environments, immediate results are rewarded, making it tempting to take shortcuts that provide quick wins but fail to contribute to long-term growth. For example, a business professional might choose to simply complete their assigned responsibilities each day, avoiding extra challenges that could expose gaps in their expertise. However, one who embraces a mastery approach might volunteer to assist a senior executive with a high-level report or presentation, even though it risks failure or critique.

By stepping into a more challenging role, they gain invaluable experience, new skills, and visibility within their organization—far outweighing the temporary safety of staying within their comfort zone. Similarly, an athlete committed to mastery may choose to compete against superior opponents, knowing they might finish last, rather than selecting an easier competition that guarantees a podium finish. While the latter might provide a confidence boost in the moment, only by testing themselves against higher competition can they identify weaknesses, improve, and reach their true potential. Those who embrace mastery understand that deep skill development takes time and that short-term setbacks are part of the process. Stay committed to the path of real growth, even when it seems slower than those chasing performance-based validation. Trust that mastery, built over time, will ultimately surpass quick and fleeting success.

Step 6. Surround Yourself with Mastery-Oriented Influences

The people and environments around you significantly impact your mindset. If you are constantly surrounded by individuals who chase quick wins, avoid challenges, or define success solely by external validation, it becomes difficult to maintain a mastery approach. Instead, seek out mentors, coaches, and peers who prioritize growth, resilience, and deep learning. These are the people who value the process of improvement over just the outcomes—those who analyze mistakes rather than hide them, embrace challenges rather than avoid them, and view effort as a tool for progress rather than a sign of weakness.

Engaging in mastery-oriented communities reinforces this mindset. Whether it's joining a professional network that emphasizes skill development over competition, training with teammates who push each other to improve rather than just win, or working under a leader who values innovation over immediate perfection, the right environment makes all the difference. For example, an aspiring entrepreneur who surrounds themselves with experienced business leaders focused on long-term sustainability will likely develop patience and strategic thinking, rather than rushing into high-risk, superficial success ventures. Similarly, an athlete training with teammates who analyze their technique and refine their approach will see greater long-term growth than one in an environment where only winning is celebrated. The more you immerse yourself in a mastery-driven culture, the more naturally this mindset will become ingrained in your approach to life.

Chapter 3 Reflection: How Goal-Orientation Affects Peak Performance

Embracing a mastery approach doesn't mean ignoring achievement—it means redefining success in a way that fuels long-term excellence. By shifting your focus to growth, persistence, and continuous learning, you create a sustainable foundation for peak performance. Whether in your career, personal goals, or athletic pursuits, adopting this orientation will not only help you achieve more but will also ensure that success is both fulfilling and lasting.

Mastering your goal orientation also has profound benefits beyond achievement. By focusing on self-improvement rather than external validation, you reduce the anxiety that often accompanies comparison and fear of failure. This mindset allows you to view setbacks as learning opportunities rather than threats to your self-worth, ultimately building powerful motivation. When you pursue progress rather than perfection, you free yourself from the pressure of constant validation, which creates a more enjoyable and sustainable journey toward your goals.

However, maintaining a mastery approach requires intentionality, especially when navigating environments that prioritize short-term performance and external benchmarks. In competitive workplaces, academic settings, or athletic competitions, the pressure to achieve quick results can seriously challenge your commitment to long-term growth. It is in these moments that the mastery approach must be purposefully maintained, reminding yourself that true excellence is built over time. By staying focused on your development, resisting the temptation to measure success solely by immediate outcomes, and surrounding yourself with mastery-oriented influences, you can cultivate a mindset that thrives regardless of external pressures. By doing so, you not only achieve peak performance but also find deeper meaning and fulfillment in your pursuit of excellence. Along the way, you'll set yourself apart as an outlier in your field while inspiring those around you with your unwavering dedication.

CHAPTER 3 ACTION ITEMS

- Assess your goal orientation and the orientation of your environment. *(Time Commitment ~ 30 minutes)*
- Develop a strategic plan to intentionally adopt a mastery mindset. *(Time Commitment ~ 1 hour)*

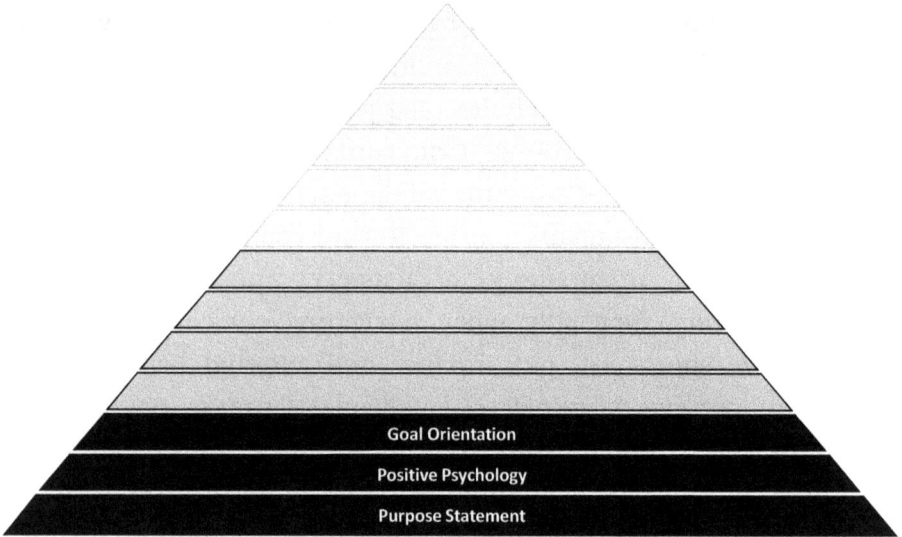

Goal Orientation

Positive Psychology

Purpose Statement

SECTION 2

FUELING YOUR MOTIVATION

STORY: FUELING YOUR AMBITION AND DRIVE

Fueling your motivation is essential for achieving extraordinary goals, especially when the journey is long and challenging. It requires more than just initial enthusiasm; it demands a strategic blend of SMART goals, volition, resilience, and grit. By setting clear and actionable steps, maintaining unwavering willpower, bouncing back from setbacks, and persevering through adversity, you can sustain your drive even when the going gets tough. The following story of Diana Nyad beautifully illustrates how these principles work together to turn dreams into reality. Her incredible journey from Cuba to Florida is a testament to the power of focused motivation and relentless determination, showing us that no goal is too ambitious when fueled by the right mindset.[20]

Diana's dream of swimming from Cuba to Florida began in her youth, but it wasn't until she was 60 years old that she set her sights on achieving it. She broke down this monumental goal into specific, measurable, achievable, relevant, and time-bound steps (a SMART Goal). Diana meticulously planned her training, nutrition, and logistics, ensuring every aspect of her preparation was aligned with her ultimate objective.

Setting the goal was just the beginning. Diana's volition, or willpower, was the driving force behind her disciplined action. She committed to a rigorous training schedule, often swimming for hours in open water to build her endurance. Even when faced with the physical and mental toll of such intense preparation, Diana's commitment never wavered. She made conscious choices every day to prioritize her goal, demonstrating the power of volition in pursuing long-term objectives.

Diana's journey was fraught with challenges. She attempted the swim multiple times, facing obstacles such as jellyfish stings, strong currents, and extreme fatigue. Each failed attempt could have been a reason to give up, but Diana's resilience shone through. She viewed each setback as a learning opportunity, adjusting her strategy and strengthening her resolve. Her ability to recover and grow from adversity was crucial in her eventual success.

Grit, the relentless perseverance and passion for long-term goals, was perhaps the most defining characteristic of Diana's journey. Despite numerous setbacks and the physical demands of the swim, Diana's passion for her goal never diminished. Her grit kept her pushing forward, even when progress seemed slow and the odds were against her. On September 2, 2013, after nearly 53 hours of continuous swimming, Diana Nyad finally achieved her dream, becoming the first person to swim from Cuba to Florida without a shark cage.

Diana Nyad's story is a powerful testament to the transformative impact of fueling your motivation through the use of these four sustaining psychological principles. Her journey to swim from Cuba to Florida demonstrates that extraordinary achievements are not merely about talent or luck but about setting clear goals, committing to disciplined action, and embracing resilience in the face of setbacks. Her unwavering determination and strategic planning remind us that peak performance is fueled by passion and perseverance, even when the path is uncertain. Whatever our meaningful pursuits might be, these principles empower us to turn ambitious dreams into remarkable achievements, ensuring that our journey is both successful and deeply fulfilling.

We know that peak performance doesn't just happen—it requires a foundation of powerful mental frameworks, resilience, and unwavering commitment. This section explores the essential elements that fuel motivation and sustain high achievement, no matter the challenges we face. By mastering these principles, you'll equip yourself with the tools necessary to transform ambition into accomplishment, pushing through setbacks and staying the course when others would give up.

This section begins by introducing SMART Goals, a practical framework developed by George Doran to transform aspirations into actionable, measurable steps. This approach ensures that your goals are not just grand intentions but strategic plans that direct your efforts and measure your progress. From there, we will explore volition, the engine behind disciplined action and conscious choices. It's not enough to set goals—you must also cultivate the willpower and commitment to pursue them, even when motivation wanes.[21]

Next, we examine resilience, the ability to recover and grow through adversity. In any pursuit of excellence, setbacks are inevitable. By developing resilience, you learn to view challenges as opportunities for growth, building mental toughness that empowers you to keep moving forward. We will then conclude this section by discussing grit—the relentless perseverance and passion that sustain long-term effort. Grit fuels your commitment to your vision, even when progress seems slow or obstacles seem insurmountable.

These chapters provide practical yet critical tools designed to help you navigate the highs and lows of your journey. By integrating SMART goals, volition, resilience, and grit into our lives, we'll build a strong foundation for peak performance. As we strive for success, these principles will empower us to achieve extraordinary results while enjoying a fulfilling and meaningful journey.

CHAPTER 4

SMART GOALS
BRIDGING AMBITION AND ACHIEVEMENT

STORY: SMART GOALS AND DETERMINATION— LIZ MURRAY'S INCREDIBLE JOURNEY

Liz Murray's life is a powerful testament to the transformative power of SMART goals. Born to drug-addicted parents in the Bronx, Liz faced unimaginable challenges from a young age. By the time she was 15, she was homeless, living on the streets, and struggling to survive. Yet, despite these hardships, Liz was determined to change her life. She set a clear and specific goal: to get an education and attend Harvard University. This goal was not only ambitious but also deeply personal, representing her desire to break free from the cycle of poverty and create a better future for herself.

To make her dream measurable and achievable, Liz broke down her goal into manageable steps. She found a stable place to stay, enrolled in high school, and focused on excelling academically. Balancing incredible challenges, she attended school during the day while working nights to support herself. Liz studied in hallways and subway stations, driven by her commitment to her dream. Her hard work paid off when she graduated in just two years with top grades and earned a scholarship from the New York Times—an achievement that showcased her dedication and effectiveness in setting clear, actionable objectives.

After high school, Liz faced the daunting task of adapting to the rigorous academic environment at Harvard University. The transition was not easy; she had to navigate a world vastly different from her previous experiences. Despite these challenges, Liz's resilience and determination helped her persevere. She embraced the opportunity to learn and grow, drawing on the same grit and volition that had propelled her through high school.

At Harvard, Liz continued to excel academically while also finding ways to reconnect with her past. She balanced her studies with personal growth, reflecting on her journey and the lessons learned from her parents' struggles. Her time at Harvard was life changing, not just in terms of education but also in her personal development. She graduated from Harvard in 2009 with a Bachelor of Science degree in Clinical Psychology. Liz's story is a powerful example of how setting SMART goals and living resiliently can lead to extraordinary achievements, even in the face of overwhelming adversity

Her goal was highly relevant to her overall mission of transforming her life. She understood that education was the key to unlocking new opportunities and breaking the cycle of poverty. By setting a time-bound deadline to complete high school within two years and apply to Harvard, Liz kept herself focused and motivated. Her journey was far from easy, but her unwavering commitment to her goal pushed her forward.

Liz Murray's dedication and perseverance provides an exceptional example that with clear, actionable objectives, we can overcome incredible odds and achieve the dreams we are passionate about. Her journey from homelessness to Harvard is a powerful reminder of the potential within each of us to create a better future through goal setting. This story illustrating the principles of SMART goals sets the stage for exploring how we, too, can bridge ambition and achievement with the information in this chapter.

DEFINITION OF A SMART GOAL

SMART goals are the bridge between ambition and achievement as they provide a structured framework that empowers you to define your objectives clearly and strategically. Unlike vague aspirations, SMART goals break down your dreams into specific, manageable steps that pave the way for real progress. This approach eliminates ambiguity, helping you to focus your efforts and maintain the momentum needed to reach your full potential. In whatever goal we are purposefully pursuing, SMART goals are the trail map to our desired realities.

The power of SMART goals lies in their strategic design, which follows five essential criteria: Specific, Measurable, Achievable, Relevant, and Time-bound. Being *Specific* means defining exactly what you want to accomplish, leaving no room for vague intentions. This clarity helps you to concentrate your resources on what truly matters. *Measurable* goals allow you to track your progress and recognize achievements along the way, keeping you motivated and accountable. *Achievable* goals are realistic yet challenging, ensuring that you stretch your abilities without setting yourself up for failure. By staying *Relevant*, your goals align with your larger purpose and values, keeping you focused on what truly matters. Finally, *Time-bound* goals create a sense of urgency, encouraging consistent action and preventing procrastination.

SMART goals provide direction, fuel your motivation, and create momentum in your life. By clearly defining each step and setting benchmarks, you can celebrate small victories, stay focused through setbacks, and adapt your approach as needed. This structure empowers you to navigate obstacles with confidence and purpose, ensuring that you remain on track even when challenges arise. In the pursuit of peak performance, SMART goals create a blueprint for turning ambitious dreams into extraordinary realities.

The Importance of Using SMART Goals for Peak Performance

SMART goals are essential for achieving peak performance because they create strategic movement. Unlike vague resolutions or unstructured intentions, SMART goals offer a well-defined blueprint that channels your energy and focus into purposeful action. They empower you to transform your aspirations into actionable steps, ensuring that your efforts are directed toward meaningful outcomes rather than getting lost in distractions. In the pursuit of peak performance, SMART goals are the difference between always dreaming of success and actively creating it.

Regular goal setting, such as New Year's resolutions or general intentions like "I want to be healthier" or "I want to be successful," often lacks the specificity needed to drive consistent progress. These types of goals are typically broad and undefined, making it difficult to measure success or stay accountable. As a result, they are extremely susceptible to failure, as they do not provide the clarity needed to navigate challenges or maintain motivation. Without specific targets or a timeline, the sense of urgency fades, and it becomes easy to lose focus or give up when obstacles arise. This approach leads to frustration and stagnation, preventing you from reaching serious outcomes.

On the other hand, having no goals at all—or simply relying on intentions, emotions, or random interests—leads to a scattered and unproductive pursuit of success. Without a clear direction, you may find yourself drifting from one opportunity to another without making significant progress. This lack of focus results in wasted time and energy, as you react to external circumstances rather than proactively shaping your future. Even with an excellent work ethic and high aptitude, this random pursuit of success will never yield more than mediocre results. While being excited about a task is valuable, it is not enough to sustain high achievement or peak performance. True success requires a strategic plan that transforms raw ambition into consistent and long-term purposeful action.

This is where SMART goals excel above typical goal-setting behaviors. By being *Specific, Measurable, Achievable, Relevant,* and *Time-bound,* SMART goals provide a detailed roadmap that keeps you focused, motivated, and accountable. They allow you to measure your progress objectively, celebrate milestones, and adjust your approach with purpose. This strategic framework empowers you to maneuver around and maintain momentum when the journey becomes challenging.

In the pursuit of peak performance, SMART goals are essential. They bridge the gap between potential and consistent, deliberate action. It is this sustained effort, guided by clear and structured goals, that elevates performance from average to exceptional. By adopting the SMART framework, you can maximize your resources, stay focused, and systematically achieve extraordinary accomplishments.

USING SMART GOALS EFFECTIVELY FOR PEAK PERFORMANCE

To achieve peak performance and rise above your peers, it's not enough to merely set goals—you must set them strategically and execute them consistently. This is where SMART goals come into play by providing a reliable framework for focusing your energy into action. Here's how to design and apply them effectively to maximize your potential.

Step 1. Start with Specificity

The first step to setting a SMART goal is to be specific about what you want to achieve. Vague goals like "I want to be promoted" lack direction. Instead, define clear objectives that outline exactly what success looks like. For example, if you're aiming for career advancement, a specific goal could be: "*I will earn a promotion to Senior Manager within the next 12 months by increasing my team's productivity by 20% through implementing new workflow strategies.*"

Specific goals eliminate ambiguity, allowing you to focus your efforts on precise actions that are meaningful to you and clearly move you closer to your vision. In your career, specificity could involve targeting particular skills, certifications, or networking opportunities that directly align with your advancement objectives.[22]

Step 2. Measure Progress with Milestones

A goal without a way to measure progress is just a wish. Therefore, we need to establish measurable criteria to track our progression and maintain motivation. This could involve setting key performance indicators (KPIs) or identifying milestones that are important to you and mark significant progress.

For example, if you're working toward mastering a new skill, such as data analytics, you might set measurable steps like:

- Complete an advanced data analytics course within three months.
- Apply new techniques to at least three projects at work by the end of the quarter.

• Present findings to leadership, aiming for at least one project to influence a strategic decision.

By quantifying progress, you can track your movement toward your objective—or identify the need for adjustments—while celebrating achievements along the way and staying motivated to remain on track.

Step 3. Ensure Goals are Achievable and Ambitious

Peak performance requires you to stretch your capabilities while remaining realistic. Goals should challenge you to push beyond your current limits, but be grounded enough to be attainable with effort and strategic planning. Consider the balance between ambition and achievability. If your goal is to transition to a leadership role, it might not be reasonable to aim for a district management position within a year, but becoming a team leader is a realistic stepping stone. A well-structured goal could be: "*I will develop my leadership skills by leading at least two high-visibility projects and attending a leadership development program within the next six months.*" This approach ensures that you're continuously growing without setting yourself up for failure or task disengagement.

Step 4. Keep Goals Relevant to Your Peak Performance Vision

SMART goals should align with your long-term vision and contribute meaningfully to where you want your peak performance to be. Ask yourself, "Will achieving this goal bring me closer to my overall purpose?"

For example, if your career vision is to become a lead engineer, relevant goals might include:

• Mastering a new programming language or technology within the next six months to enhance your technical expertise.

- Leading two high-impact projects over the next year to demonstrate leadership and problem-solving abilities.

Relevant goals help you prioritize your efforts, ensuring that every step taken is purposeful, makes the best use of your time and resources, and aligns with your ultimate aspirations.

Step 5. Set Time-Bound Deadlines to Drive Momentum

Deadlines create urgency and prevent stagnation and complacency. By setting specific time frames, you're more likely to stay focused and engaged with your task. Ensure your timeline is realistic yet challenging enough to require maintained momentum.

For instance, if your goal is to enhance your public speaking skills, a time-bound version would be: *"I will complete a public speaking course within the next 90 days and deliver at least three presentations at team meetings within six months."*

This approach encourages consistent progress and helps you maintain accountability.

Step 6. Apply SMART Goals across Life Domains for Peak Performance

To truly rise above your peer group and achieve peak performance, consider applying SMART goals across various life domains:

- **Career Advancement:** Set specific goals for skill development, leadership roles, or professional networking within your organization. This positions you for promotions and greater influence.
- **Health and Well-being:** Peak performance isn't just about productivity—physical health and mental resilience are equally important. Establish goals for fitness, nutrition, and mindfulness practices to maintain the energy and focus needed for high performance.

- **Personal Development:** Enhance emotional intelligence, communication skills, or creative thinking. These attributes increase adaptability and problem-solving abilities, setting you apart professionally.
- **Financial Growth:** Secure financial stability through strategic investments, proactive savings, and career-related income growth goals.

By strategically applying SMART goals across multiple areas of life, you build a robust foundation that supports peak performance holistically. This approach helps you avoid being derailed by blind spots such as relationship challenges, chronic illness, or financial stress.[22]

Example of Peak Performance through SMART Goals
Consider the example of a mid-level professional aiming to secure a site lead position within two years. By leveraging SMART goals, they might establish the following:

- **Specific:** Develop expertise in advanced project management to effectively lead larger teams.
- **Measurable:** Earn the Project Management Professional (PMP) certification and lead three major cross-functional projects within 18 months.
- **Achievable:** Dedicate five hours per week to PMP study while maintaining current work responsibilities.
- **Relevant:** This goal directly supports the leadership qualifications needed for advancement in their industry.
- **Time-bound:** Secure the promotion within two years.

By taking this strategic approach, they not only enhance their skills but also position themselves as strong candidates for leadership roles, significantly increasing their chances of outperforming their peers. If promoted, they will be equipped with the necessary skills and experience to transition smoothly into the role without excessive anxiety or stress. Alternatively, if they do not receive the promotion, they will be better prepared to excel in their current role, reducing perceived stress and enhancing their overall sense of well-being.

CHAPTER 4 REFLECTION: WHY SMART GOALS ARE ESSENTIAL FOR PEAK PERFORMANCE

SMART goals provide the structure and strategic focus necessary to harness your full potential. They transform dreams into actionable steps, ensuring consistent progress and growth. Without SMART goals, ambitions remain vague and unproductive, often leading to burnout or stagnation.

Regular goal-setting methods, such as New Year's resolutions or wishful thinking, lack the precision needed to sustain momentum and achieve peak performance. Similarly, vague intentions or random pursuits lead to scattered effort and wasted potential. SMART goals counteract these pitfalls by providing clarity, accountability, and a clear path to success.

To achieve peak performance and rise above average, strategic goal-setting is crucial. SMART goals not only guide your ambitions but also fuel the discipline, motivation, and consistency required to achieve them. By designing and applying SMART goals effectively across all areas of your life, you create a comprehensive plan for extraordinary success. Embrace the power of SMART goals and watch as they transform your potential into peak performance.

CHAPTER 4 ACTION ITEMS

- Create SMART goals for the declarative statements of your purpose statement. *(Time Commitment ~ 1 hour)*

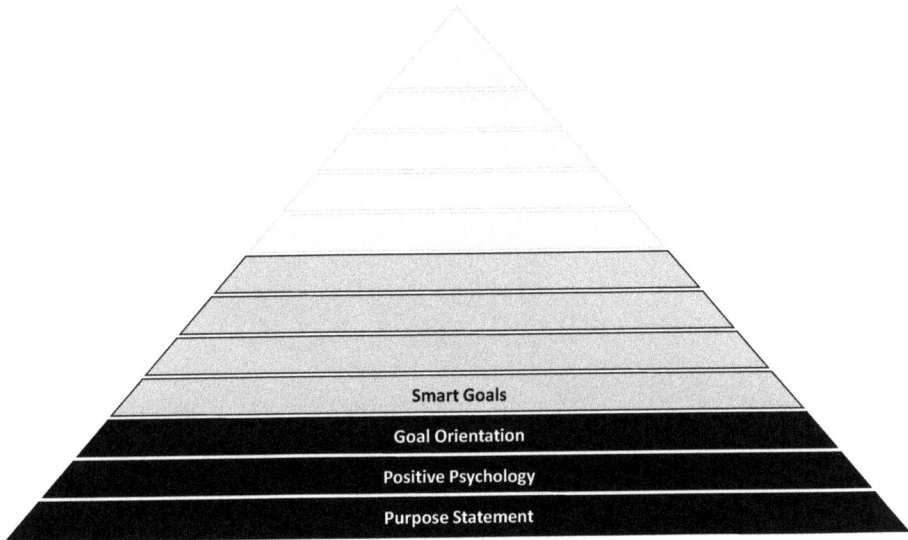

Smart Goals

Goal Orientation

Positive Psychology

Purpose Statement

CHAPTER 5
VOLITION
FUELING MOTIVATION BY HARNESSING PASSION

STORY: THE TRANSFORMATIVE POWER OF VOLITION

In regards to peak performance, few stories exemplify the power of volition—the fusion of passion, discipline, and conscious choice—better than that of Wilma Rudolph. Born prematurely in 1940 in Tennessee, Wilma faced a series of health challenges early in life, including polio, which left her with a paralyzed left leg. Doctors doubted she would ever walk without braces, let alone run.

However, Wilma's indomitable spirit refused to accept this prognosis. With unwavering determination, she committed to a rigorous regimen of physical therapy, often enduring pain and fatigue. Her family's support and her own relentless willpower fueled her progress. By the age of 12, she had shed her braces and began to pursue athletics, driven by a passion for running.

Wilma's journey was far from easy. She faced not only physical hurdles but also the societal challenges of racial segregation and gender inequality prevalent in mid-20th-century America. Yet, her disciplined approach to training and her conscious choice to persevere propelled her forward.

Her hard work culminated in a historic performance at the 1960 Rome Olympics, where she became the first American woman to win three gold medals in track and field during a single Olympic Games. She won gold in the 100-meter dash, tying the world record at 11.3 seconds, and set a new Olympic record in the 200-meter dash with a time of 23.2 seconds. Additionally, she anchored the U.S. team to victory in the 4x100-meter relay, setting a world record of 44.4 seconds in the semifinals.

Wilma's achievements shattered records and stereotypes, inspiring generations to come. She was acclaimed as the fastest woman in the world during the 1960s and became an international sports icon. Her story is a testament to the transformative power of volition. Her conscious choices, disciplined training, and unwavering willpower not only enabled her to overcome personal and societal obstacles but also to reach extraordinary heights in her athletic career. Her legacy continues to inspire those striving for peak performance, demonstrating that with steadfast volition, even the most daunting challenges can be overcome.

DEFINITION OF VOLITION

Volition is the psychological fuel that gives our actions stamina, driving us to pursue our goals even when motivation wanes and obstacles arise. Central to volition is our willpower to transform intentions into deliberate action through the force of determination, discipline, and conscious choice. Unlike short bursts of motivation or emotional impulses, volition is a sustained, strategic commitment to follow through on your goals, no matter the circumstances. It is the mental engine that pushes you to wake up early for that workout, continue studying after fatigue sets in, or resist distractions to focus on meaningful work. In essence, volition bridges the gap between setting a goal and pushing it across the finish line, aligning our purpose and action.

The power of volition lies in its ability to overcome barriers that derail most people's efforts, such as procrastination, temptation, or fatigue. It is our discipline that empowers us to make decisions that align with our long-term vision, even when short-term pleasures beckon. This conscious control over behavior requires self-regulation and a deep sense of personal agency—the belief that you have the power to influence your outcomes through your actions. For example, when faced with a difficult challenge, someone with strong volition doesn't just rely on initial enthusiasm or motivation; they draw on their disciplined willpower to keep taking steps forward, actively choosing perseverance over surrender. This is why volition is often seen as the cornerstone of peak performance and extraordinary achievement.

While motivation is essential for getting started, it is inherently unstable and often influenced by external factors, such as praise, rewards, or even the weather. Volition, however, is unwavering less volatile because it is rooted in conscious choice, inner drive, and personal responsibility. It is the mental contract you make with yourself to pursue your goals relentlessly, regardless of external circumstances or internal doubts. This makes volition especially powerful in the face of setbacks, as it equips you with the mental resilience needed to persist through adversity. It allows you to push beyond your comfort zone, embrace discomfort as part of the growth process, and ultimately rise above mediocrity.

The beauty of volition lies in its accessibility—everyone has the potential to cultivate it. Unlike talent or intelligence, which may be unevenly distributed, volition is a skill that can be developed through practice and intentional effort. It begins with making conscious choices that align with your values and long-term vision, then reinforcing those choices through disciplined action. By understanding and harnessing the power of volition, you can unlock the secret to extraordinary success, transforming your dreams into reality one deliberate, goal-congruent step at a time.

THE IMPORTANCE OF VOLITION FOR PEAK PERFORMANCE

Peak performance requires consistently taking the right actions to transform ambition into reality. This is where volition becomes indispensable. Volition is a special character strength that separates the ordinary from the extraordinary. It is the driving force that empowers you to keep moving forward when motivation fades, obstacles arise, and the path to success becomes difficult. Unlike momentary inspiration, volition is a relentless commitment to pursue our purpose. When harnessed effectively, volition not only fuels your drive but also propels you to achieve a level of performance that most people will not commit to.

Volition uniquely influences peak performance by fostering unwavering commitment. This goes beyond merely setting goals; it involves cultivating a mindset that embraces discomfort, uncertainty, and adversity as essential parts of the journey. High achievers understand that the pursuit of excellence is not always exciting or glamorous—it often involves grueling effort, tedious repetition, and sacrifice. Volition gives you the mental toughness to push through these challenges, maintaining focus and discipline even when the initial excitement has long worn off. This commitment to goal-congruent action, regardless of emotional state or external circumstances, is what allows peak performers to maintain their edge and consistently outperform their peers.

One of the most powerful aspects of volition is its ability to convert obstacles into opportunities for growth. When faced with setbacks, most people either lose momentum or give up, but those with strong volition use these challenges as fuel to improve and adapt. They consciously choose to see failure not as a dead-end but as a performance indicator toward mastery. This tenacious mindset not only enhances performance but also accelerates personal and professional development. By harnessing volition, you can navigate adversity with confidence, maintain strategic focus, and continue progressing toward your goals, no matter the difficulties encountered along the way. It is this mindset that sets you apart from your peer group.

Cultivating volition also fosters a sense of agency and personal responsibility, which is crucial for peak performance. It empowers you to take control of your actions, decisions, and ultimately, your destiny. Rather than being at the mercy of external circumstances or current level of motivation, you become the architect of your own success, making deliberate choices that align with your purpose statement. This self-directed approach creates an unshakable sense of empowerment, driving you to persevere with passion and intensity. When you realize that every action is a conscious choice, you unlock an extraordinary level of potential and break free from limitations that hold others back.

To achieve peak performance and rise above mediocrity, volition is essential. It is the backbone of consistent effort, strategic persistence, and reliable focus. By cultivating and harnessing this powerful psychological construct, you gain the power to defy odds, break through barriers, and turn your boldest dreams into extraordinary achievements. Embracing volition allows you to ambitiously pursue your goals no matter how challenging or distant they may seem. Throughout your journey, volition will be the force that ensures you never stop moving forward.

EFFECTIVELY CULTIVATING AND APPLYING VOLITION FOR PEAK PERFORMANCE

Volition is a powerful driving force behind peak performance and transforms our intentions into actions. It's not an innate trait but a skill we can cultivate through deliberate practice. When effectively applied, volition becomes a powerful engine that drives consistent progress, strategic decision-making, and unwavering perseverance toward our goals, regardless of setbacks or obstacles.[21] Here's how to cultivate and deploy this character strength to achieve extraordinary peak performance.

Step 1. Master Your Mindset with Self-Awareness

Peak performers understand that every action starts with a choice to take that action. To make intentional, purpose-driven decisions, you must first master your mindset through heightened self-awareness. Begin by reflecting on your daily routines to identify when you lose focus or motivation. Use mindfulness practices to observe your thought patterns and emotional triggers. This isn't just about noticing distractions; it's about understanding why and when they occur. By mastering self-awareness, you empower yourself to make conscious choices that align with your goals and eliminate self-sabotaging habits. This foundational step puts you in the driver's seat of your outcomes, paving the way for intentional, purpose-driven action.

Step 2. Forge Unbreakable Willpower despite Daily Challenges

Willpower isn't just a character strength; it's a muscle that grows stronger with practice. To cultivate unbreakable willpower, consistently challenge yourself with tasks that require discipline. Start with small, manageable goals, such as waking up an hour earlier, sticking to a workout routine, or practicing focused work sessions at specific times without distractions. These seemingly minor victories accumulate, building your capacity for self-control and enhancing your ability to persist through discomfort. Additionally, practice delayed gratification by refusing immediate temptations in favor of long-term rewards. Each time you overcome a challenge, you strengthen your mental resilience, enabling you to stay focused on your priorities even when distractions arise. This disciplined practice is the cornerstone of volition, transforming sporadic motivation into unwavering determination.

Step 3. Design an Unstoppable Environment for Success

Willpower is a finite resource that can be depleted by constant decision-making or exposure to distractions. To maximize your volition, design an environment that propels you toward success. Remove temptations, organize your workspace, and structure your day to minimize decision fatigue. For example, set specific times for focused work, schedule regular breaks, and prepare meals in advance to avoid impulsive eating. By automating routine tasks and creating habits that align with your goals, you conserve willpower for high-impact actions. This strategic approach eliminates unnecessary confrontations, allowing you to channel your volition into meaningful pursuits. When surrounded by the right environment, achieving success becomes significantly more efficient and attainable.

Step 4. Use Mental Rehearsal to Boost Your Volition

Visualization is a powerful tool for anyone striving for peak performance. Supercharge your volition by regularly practicing mental rehearsal. Anticipate the obstacles or triggers you may encounter, and develop strategies to overcome them. This mental practice, often referred to as an *implementation intention*, reduces uncertainty, increases confidence, and strengthens your commitment to action, making it easier to stay motivated when challenges do arise. To maximize effectiveness, visualize the process as well as the outcome, focusing on the action, effort, resilience, and discipline required to reach your goal. By mentally rehearsing for success, you prime your mind for victory, ensuring that your actions follow the strategy you've already planned when expected obstacles or distractions are inevitably encountered.[23]

Step 5. Fortify Your Resolve with Support

Even the most determined individuals need support, especially when faced with a prolonged period of setbacks. Fortify your resolve by building a network of accountability partners who inspire you to stay committed to your purpose. Share your goals with trusted mentors, colleagues, or friends who will provide constructive feedback, encouragement, and honest assessments of your progress. Surround yourself with high achievers and like-minded individuals who kindly challenge you and keep you growing. By creating a sense of responsibility to others, you reinforce your commitment to your goals. This powerful social contract fuels your volition, ensuring that you persist even when internal motivation wavers. With the right support system, quitting fades as an option.

Step 6. Recharge with Strategic Recovery

Volition isn't about relentless effort without rest; it requires sustainable action and strategic recovery. Recharge your mental and physical energy by scheduling regular breaks, prioritizing sleep, and engaging in activities that rejuvenate you. Equally important is practicing self-compassion to navigate setbacks without self-criticism. Understand that failures are part of the growth process and use them as opportunities to learn and adapt. By cultivating a positive mindset and practicing self-compassion, you safeguard your willpower and sustain long-term motivation, ensuring your overall well-being. This strategic balance prevents burnout and ensures that you're always ready to take on the next challenge with renewed and sustained vigor.

Step 7. Use Consistent Application to Achieve Extraordinary Outcomes

Cultivating volition isn't an erratic effort—it's about consistent application and deliberate practice. As you develop stronger willpower, conscious decision-making, and strategic discipline, you'll experience a compounding effect on your performance from your perseverance. Each deliberate action builds momentum, fostering a habit of persistence that becomes second nature. Over time, this cultivated volition enables you to achieve extraordinary goals that once seemed impossible, rising above peers who rely solely on talent or short-lived motivation. By consistently applying these strategies, you will develop the mental toughness, discipline, and fortitude to ambitiously and confidently pursue your goals, leading to extraordinary outcomes.

CHAPTER 5 REFLECTION: THE POWER OF VOLITION ON PEAK PERFORMANCE

Extraordinary achievers master their mindset through self-awareness, forge unbreakable willpower through disciplined choices, and eliminate distractions by designing strategic environments. They visualize success, leverage accountability, and prioritize recovery to sustain their momentum. By cultivating habits of volition, they gain the power to persevere when others quit and to turn their ambitions into extraordinary accomplishments.

Remember, as you pursue your most meaningful goals, setbacks and disappointments are inevitable. Yet, by harnessing volition as one of your driving forces, you can rise above those challenges with relentless tenacity, continually pushing your goals forward until you cross the finish line.

CHAPTER 5 ACTION ITEMS

- Design an environment that ignites enthusiasm for your purpose statement. *(Time Commitment ~ 1 hour)*
- Develop, practice, and execute an implementation strategy to strengthen your willpower and safeguard your goal from distractions or short-term temptations. *(Time Commitment ~ 1 hour)*

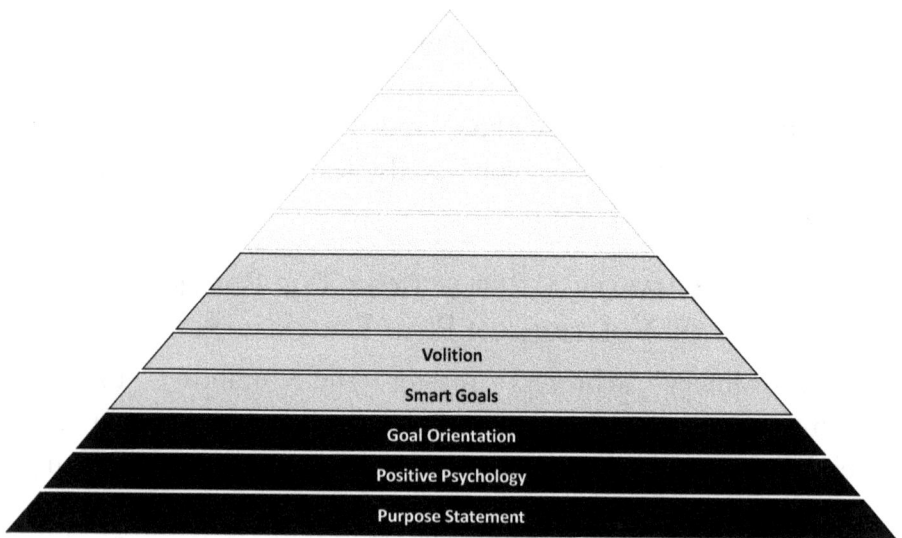

Volition

Smart Goals

Goal Orientation

Positive Psychology

Purpose Statement

CHAPTER 6

RESILIENCE
GROWING THROUGH ADVERSITY

STORY: USING ADVERSITY FOR EXTRAORDINARY SUCCESS

On a normal October morning in 2003, 13-year-old Bethany Hamilton paddled out into the pristine waters off Kauai, Hawaii, ready for another perfect day of surfing. While pursuing her goal of becoming a professional surfer, she had spent most of her young life chasing waves, training relentlessly, and pushing herself to the limits of her ability. But in a matter of seconds, her world changed forever.

Out of nowhere, a 14-foot tiger shark struck, biting off her left arm in a violent attack. Rushed to the hospital in critical condition, Bethany lost over 60% of her blood and barely survived. Her dream of becoming a competitive surfer now seemed impossible. How could she balance on a board with one arm? How could she find the courage to paddle back into the ocean after such a traumatic attack? Most would have surrendered to fear, grief, and the weight of their new limitations. But Bethany was different—she drew from deep reservoirs of resilience, refusing to let adversity define her future.

Instead of succumbing to despair, she focused on what she could control. Through sheer resilience, she adapted to her new reality. She learned to surf again, experimenting with different techniques and refusing to accept limitations. Just one month after the attack, she was back in the water. Less than two years later, she won a national surfing championship.

Bethany's story isn't just about surviving a tragedy—it's about transforming hardship into fuel for growth. Since she couldn't avoid adversity; she embraced it, proving that resilience is a key tool that separates those who quit from adversity from those who grow from hardship. Today, she's a world-class professional surfer, a bestselling author, and an inspiration to millions. Her journey exemplifies the core of resilience: the ability to rise after being knocked down, to find strength in the struggle, and to turn unwanted setbacks into stepping stones for success.

As we explore resilience in this chapter, Bethany's story demonstrates that challenges don't have to be framed as roadblocks but can be used as opportunities to grow stronger. The waves of life will always be crashing down on us—but it's those who get back up and keep riding that achieve peak performance.

DEFINITION OF RESILIENCE

Resilience is the psychological strength that allows you to adapt, recover, and thrive in the face of adversity. It is not about avoiding hardship but about responding to challenges in ways that foster personal growth and long-term success. Specifically, resilience is the skill to maintain emotional balance, learn from setbacks, and leverage internal and external resources to navigate difficult experiences.

Resilient individuals do not simply endure struggles—they actively transform them into stepping stones for greater achievement. This ability to remain steadfast under pressure fosters emotional well-being, sharpens critical thinking, and enhances adaptability. More importantly, resilience serves as a powerful protective factor against helplessness, a key risk factor for anxiety and depression. When faced with obstacles, those lacking resilience may succumb to hopelessness, feeling powerless to change their circumstances. In contrast, resilient individuals cultivate persistence and self-efficacy, allowing them to view setbacks as temporary and solvable rather than insurmountable. By maintaining optimism, they protect their mental health, enabling them to navigate challenges without becoming overwhelmed by fear or self-doubt.[9]

The benefits of resilience extend far beyond mental toughness. It strengthens physical health, deepens social connections, and empowers individuals to sustain motivation in the pursuit of academic, professional, and personal excellence. Resilience fosters a sense of balance, helping individuals stay focused on their goals rather than being derailed by discouragement. While others may fall into despair and quit when faced with hardship, resilient individuals press forward, using adversity as fuel for growth. Ultimately, resilience is a critical driving force behind sustained success and long-term fulfillment in the event of serious hardships, allowing you to turn setbacks into setups for peak performance.

THE IMPORTANCE OF RESILIENCE FOR PEAK PERFORMANCE

Peak performance certainly requires persistence, but it often demands the ability to rise from the ashes when everything falls apart. True resilience emerges in the face of extreme adversity when setbacks are so profound that they threaten to derail everything we have worked toward. It is in these moments—when plans collapse, confidence is shaken, and the path forward seems impossible—that the resilience construct is needed to help us reevaluate, adapt, and forge a new way forward. Unlike mere persistence, which pushes forward on the same track despite difficulties, resilience demands a deeper transformation. It separates those who are crushed by devastating obstacles—left deflated, defeated, and unable to move forward—from those who refuse to let failure define them. Resilient individuals do not simply keep going; they reimagine their approach, creatively rebuilding their strategy with renewed determination. They rise, not by stubbornly clinging to a broken plan, but by having the courage to pivot, innovate, and forge a new path toward success.

A key component of resilience is self-efficacy—the confidence in one's skills and ability to influence outcomes and overcome challenges. High levels of self-efficacy lead to increased motivation, improved problem-solving, and a greater willingness to take calculated risks, all of which are essential for peak performance. When individuals trust their ability to navigate difficulties, they are more likely to push beyond their perceived limits. Athletes, entrepreneurs, and top professionals cultivate this inner confidence, using it to maintain composure and focus when the stakes are high. Without self-efficacy, challenges can feel insurmountable, leading to hesitation and self-doubt that can derail progress.

Optimism, another crucial element of resilience, plays a significant role in sustaining high performance. Resilient individuals maintain a positive outlook, seeing failures as opportunities to learn rather than as definitive defeats. This mindset fosters adaptability, creativity, and persistence, allowing them to continuously refine their skills and strategies. Optimism also protects against burnout by reducing the emotional toll of setbacks, ensuring that individuals stay motivated even in the face of adversity. Those who embrace an optimistic perspective are better equipped to maintain momentum when pursuing ambitious goals, while those who focus on negativity are much more likely to give up prematurely.

Resilience also enhances peak performance by partnering with grit—the sustained passion and perseverance needed to achieve long-term success. Gritty individuals do not rely on fleeting motivation; they commit to their goals despite obstacles, failures, or slow progress. This relentless drive allows them to develop expertise and master their craft over time. Additionally, resilience helps maintain emotional balance, preventing stress from undermining performance. By reducing anxiety and depression, resilience ensures that mental clarity and energy remain intact, allowing individuals to stay engaged, make strategic decisions, and execute at their highest level.[24]

Finally, gratitude—often overlooked as a performance-enhancing trait—serves as a powerful resilience booster. When individuals practice gratitude, they shift their focus away from frustrations, self-pity, and setbacks, reinforcing a mindset of abundance rather than deficiency. This perspective fuels resilience by increasing emotional regulation, strengthening social connections, and promoting a sense of purpose. Those who cultivate gratitude are more likely to remain resilient under pressure, using their appreciation for progress and support systems as motivation to keep striving despite some disappointments.

Resilience serves as the safeguard of peak performance, shielding individuals from the derailment that adversity and disappointment usually bring. While we rarely anticipate devastating setbacks on the path to achieving what we are passionate about, they arise far more often than expected. Profound obstacles are not welcomed, yet they are nearly inevitable for those striving to become outliers in their field.

In these moments—when hope dwindles and catastrophe appears unavoidable—resilience becomes the critical tool that allows us to recalibrate, adapt, and push forward with renewed determination, transforming what seems like an ending into a new beginning.

EFFECTIVELY CULTIVATING AND APPLYING RESILIENCE FOR PEAK PERFORMANCE

Peak performance is not a rare burst of excellence or a lucky break—it is a consistent, high-level execution of skill and effort over time. It is marked by reliability, precision, and the ability to perform at one's best under varying conditions. Unlike average performance, which is easily influenced by external factors such as motivation, mood, or environment, peak performance requires discipline, focus, and the capacity to sustain excellence even in the face of setbacks. However, no matter how skilled or prepared an individual is, adversity is inevitable—unexpected failures, major disappointments, and moments of self-doubt can threaten to disrupt progress. This is where resilience becomes essential, acting as the stabilizing force that keeps performance on track and prevents temporary setbacks from becoming permanent barriers.[20, 25]

To make resilience a dependable trait in your character, follow these key steps to cultivate and apply it to achieve peak performance:

Step 1. Develop a Growth Mindset

Resilience starts with how we perceive challenges. Adopting a mastery or growth mindset—believing that abilities and intelligence can be developed through effort—allows us to see setbacks as learning experiences rather than failures. Embracing obstacles as opportunities for improvement naturally strengthens our ability to persist through difficulties, fostering a mindset that views setbacks as necessary steps toward becoming extraordinary. Individuals with this mindset understand that failure is not a detour but essential feedback, providing valuable insights into what works and what doesn't. By analyzing challenges objectively rather than emotionally, you can make strategic adjustments and continue progressing toward your goal without losing momentum. Remember to anticipate mistakes as stepping stones toward greater competence.

This growth-focused approach shifts the focus from avoiding failure to extracting valuable insights from every struggle. Setbacks become feedback mechanisms, highlighting areas for improvement and offering clues to refine strategies for future success. Mastery-driven individuals are more adaptable and less likely to be derailed by disappointment. This approach transforms temporary failures into fuel for growth, reinforcing resilience and long-term success. By expecting and embracing challenges, those with a mastery mindset develop unshakable confidence in their ability to improve, knowing that the response to setbacks creates their potential.

Step 2. Strengthen Self-Efficacy

Confidence in your ability to complete tasks and drive your outcomes grows your self-efficacy through the relentless pursuit of mastery. As you refine your skills and sharpen your problem-solving abilities through rigorous training in your field, you develop the confidence to navigate unexpected challenges. Every challenging success or breakthrough in understanding enhances your competence, turning delays in your journey into opportunities for important growth and fortifying your resilience.

Mastery experiences—witnessing your successes in overcoming difficulties—serve as undeniable proof of your capabilities, solidifying your belief in yourself. Surrounding yourself with skilled peers, seeking mentorship, and learning from experts further enhance your self-efficacy, while maintaining an optimistic mindset helps sustain confidence under pressure. The more proficient you become, the more adaptable and resilient you feel, approaching obstacles not with hesitation, but with the assurance that you can find innovative solutions to any challenge.

Step 3. Master Emotional and Self-Regulation

Emotional regulation is essential for peak performance, ensuring that emotions are aligned for the task rather than hindering. Stress, frustration, and self-doubt can easily derail progress if left unmitigated, but learning to manage them allows you to remain composed under pressure. Techniques such as mindfulness help you stay present, deep breathing calms physiological responses to stress, and cognitive reframing shifts negative thoughts into productive perspectives. By gaining control over your emotions, you cultivate mental clarity and prevent momentary setbacks from turning into long-term obstacles.[26]

Relatedly, self-regulation goes a step beyond emotional control, encompassing the ability to direct your thoughts, behaviors, and impulses toward long-term success. Maintaining discipline in the face of adversity requires intentional strategies such as setting clear priorities, breaking overwhelming tasks into manageable steps, and using structured processes to ensure consistent outcomes. Additionally, self-regulation includes effectively avoiding distractions—personal or environmental. Developing self-regulation means recognizing how to effectively push forward with intensity as well as when to pause for recovery, ensuring sustained performance without burnout.

Mastering both emotional regulation and self-regulation strengthens resilience, enabling you to face adversity with calmness and confidence instead of fear. When challenges arise, emotional stability helps prevent panic, while self-regulation provides the discipline needed to maintain an effective approach and persevere through tasks. Together, these skills create a foundation of steadfast composure, ensuring that obstacles become temporary detours rather than roadblocks to success.

Step 4. Build a Support Network

Resilience will struggle in isolation. Strong social connections and organizational support—whether mentors, teammates, trusted friends, or family—are crucial for building and maintaining resilience. These connections provide encourage-ment, perspective, and accountability when adversity strikes. Emotional support from a network helps reduce stress and anxiety, allowing you to approach problems with a clear mind and positive attitude. Seeking support does not indicate weakness; rather, it reinforces your ability to withstand chal-lenges and emerge stronger, showing that you are proactive in managing your well-being.

In addition to emotional support, a strong network can provide practical assistance, such as offering help, sharing resources, or providing collaborative feedback. This practi-cal support helps you stay on track and maintain momentum toward your goals. Ultimately, resilience is not just about indi-vidual strength; it's about the collective strength that comes from being part of a supportive community. By building and nurturing these connections, you create a foundation that allows you to face adversity with confidence and achieve peak performance.

Step 5. Cultivate Optimism and Gratitude

Optimism fuels resilience by helping you maintain faith in a positive outcome, even when faced with setbacks. When you approach challenges with an optimistic mindset, you are more likely to see potential solutions and opportunities rather than just obstacles. This positive outlook can boost your problem-solving abilities and keep you motivated to push through difficult times. Optimism also helps you recover more quickly from setbacks, as you are less likely to dwell on the negative and more likely to focus on what you can do to improve the situation. By maintaining a hopeful attitude, you can sustain your energy and enthusiasm, which are essential for achieving peak performance.

Similarly, gratitude shifts your focus from what is going wrong to what is still within your control, keeping your motivation intact. Practicing gratitude helps you recognize and appreciate the positive aspects of your life, even in the midst of challenges. This important shift in perspective can reduce feelings of frustration and helplessness, making it easier to stay resilient. Gratitude also fosters a sense of contentment and well-being, which can enhance your overall mental and emotional health. By regularly acknowledging the things you are thankful for, you create a buffer against stress and negativity, allowing you to maintain a balanced and positive outlook. Together, optimism and gratitude prevent discouragement from taking root and help to enhance resilience and peak performance over time.

Step 6. Commit to Adaptability

True resilience is not just about enduring hardship—it's also about adjusting your approach when necessary. The most successful individuals recognize when a plan is failing and have the flexibility to pivot without losing sight of their ultimate goal. By embracing change rather than resisting it, you ensure that temporary setbacks do not become permanent failures. Being adaptable means staying open-minded and willing to consider new ideas and perspectives, rather than clinging to a rigid, neurotic viewpoint. This openness allows you to see opportunities for improvement and growth that you might otherwise miss.

Additionally, don't be afraid to accept something better when considering feedback. Constructive criticism can provide valuable insights and help you refine your strategies. By being receptive to feedback, you demonstrate a commitment to continuous improvement and a willingness to evolve. This mindset not only enhances your resilience but also positions you to achieve peak performance. Remember, adaptability is a key component of resilience, and by staying flexible and open to change, you can navigate challenges more effectively and reach your goals with greater ease.

Step 7. Maintain Purpose and Long-Term Vision

Resilience thrives when anchored in a meaningful purpose. Knowing your "*why*" fuels perseverance, making it easier to endure short-term hardships in pursuit of long-term success. When your vision is clear and deeply personal, your commitment to your goal remains stronger than the difficulties you face. It's essential to objectively understand your purpose, as this clarity allows you to make informed decisions and course corrections when adversity is encountered. By regularly reflecting on your purpose, you can ensure that your actions continue to align with your long-term vision, keeping you motivated and focused.

Moreover, maintaining a long-term vision helps you stay resilient by providing a sense of direction and meaning.

When challenges arise, having a clear purpose enables you to see beyond immediate disappointment and stay committed to your ultimate goals. This perspective helps you navigate difficulties with a sense of confidence and determination. Additionally, a well-defined purpose allows you to evaluate your progress objectively and make necessary adjustments to your plans. By staying true to your vision and being willing to adapt, you can overcome obstacles more effectively and continue moving forward toward success. Remember, a strong sense of purpose is the foundation of resilience and long-term achievement.

Chapter 6 Reflection: Why Resilience is Foundational for Peak Performance

As you finish this chapter on resilience, remember that while peak performance certainly requires perseverance, it often requires the ability to rise again when everything seems to fall apart. True resilience shines in moments of profound adversity, when setbacks threaten to undo everything you've worked for. It's in these moments that resilience empowers you to pause, reassess, and transform setbacks into stepping stones. Resilient individuals don't just recover—they innovate, adapt, and rebuild their path with renewed determination and creativity.

Resilience is your ultimate safeguard, the armor that protects you from being derailed by life's inevitable challenges. It ensures that temporary failures remain just that—temporary— while keeping you firmly on the path to your greatest achievements. By embracing resilience, you develop the strength, courage, and flexibility to overcome any obstacle and reach your highest potential. Let resilience be your foundation, your compass, and your catalyst for turning adversity into inspiration and triumph.

Chapter 6 Action Items

- Reflect on the importance of completing your purpose statement, no matter the obstacles and setbacks you encounter. Recognize why your purpose statement is so important to you. *(Time Commitment ~ 1 hour)*

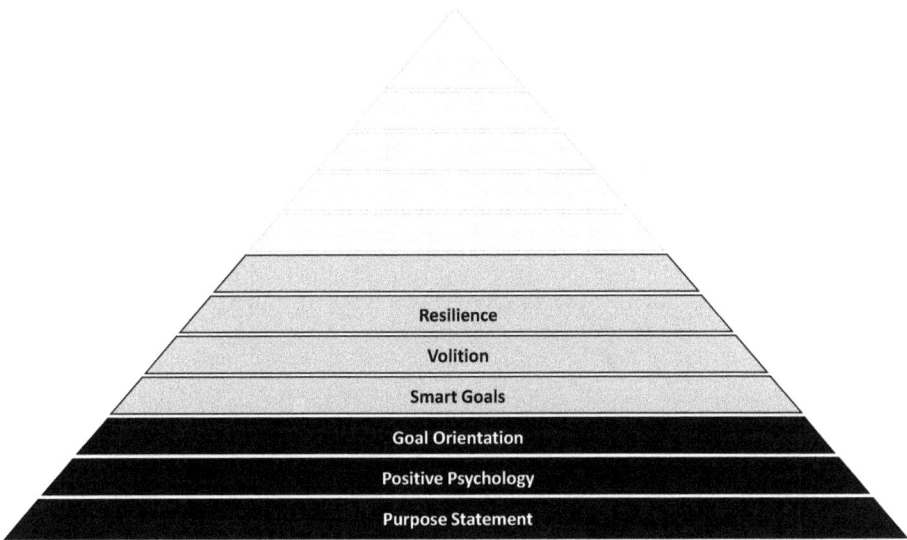

Resilience

Volition

Smart Goals

Goal Orientation

Positive Psychology

Purpose Statement

CHAPTER 7

GRIT

THE BACKBONE OF SUSTAINED EFFORT AND ACHIEVEMENT

STORY: THE UNBREAKABLE SPIRIT OF JOHN AKHWARI

In 1968, during the Mexico City Olympics, long after the marathon had been won and the stadium lights had dimmed, a lone runner entered the arena. John Stephen Akhwari of Tanzania, battered and limping from a severe fall earlier in the race, pressed forward with unwavering determination. His knee was dislocated, his body dehydrated, and every step sent a sharp wave of pain through his legs. Spectators who had remained in the stadium rose to their feet, watching in stunned silence as he hobbled the final lap toward the finish line.

When asked later why he had continued despite having no chance of winning, Akhwari's response was simple, yet profound: *"My country did not send me 5,000 miles to start the race. They sent me 5,000 miles to finish it."*

While this moment defined Akhwari in the eyes of the world, it was not a singular act of perseverance—it was the culmination of a lifetime of *grit*. Many remember the battered runner finishing last in the Olympics, but few realize he was a world-class athlete who had spent years building his endurance, discipline, and tenacity. Before the 1968 Olympics, he won the African Marathon Championships, and two years later, he finished fifth at the Commonwealth Games marathon with a blazing time of 2:15:05. He regularly ran elite-level marathons in the 2:20 range and competed fiercely in the 10,000-meter race, finishing just 30 seconds behind the leaders at the same Commonwealth Games. Akhwari didn't just show up—he put in the work year after year, never allowing setbacks to define him.

His commitment extended far beyond his own career. He returned to his village in Tanzania, where he and his wife worked tirelessly as farmers, embodying the same perseverance in daily life that he had displayed on the track. In 1983, he was awarded the National Hero Medal of Honor, a testament to his impact not just as an athlete but as an enduring symbol of grit to his country and even to the world. Later, he lent his name to the *John Stephen Akhwari Athletic Foundation*, helping train future Tanzanian Olympians. Decades after his famous race, he was invited to the 2000 Sydney Olympics and later appeared in Beijing as a goodwill ambassador, carrying the Olympic torch through Dar es Salaam in 2008.

Akhwari's legacy demonstrates that grit is more than just finishing a long race—it is about sustained effort, lifelong commitment, and an unshakable belief in the pursuit of excellence. Grit is not just about pushing through pain in a single moment; it is about showing up again and again, training long after the applause has faded, and giving your best whether the world is watching or not. It is what fuels peak performance, not just in competition but in every aspect of life, whether on the field or in the workplace.

DEFINITION OF GRIT

Grit is a psychological construct that combines passion and perseverance in the pursuit of long-term goals. Since motivation often only offers short bursts of effort, grit must be deployed for sustained commitment, resilience in the face of adversity, and an unwavering focus on personal or professional aspirations. Psychologist Angela Duckworth, who pioneered the study of grit, describes it as the ability to maintain effort and interest over the years despite failures, setbacks, and plateaus in progress. Those with grit do not merely set goals—they persist through challenges, refining their strategies, and maintaining their determination even when success is not immediate.

However, several risk factors can undermine grit and make it difficult for individuals to sustain their long-term efforts. A lack of clear goals, for instance, can lead to aimlessness, making perseverance difficult when obstacles arise. A fixed mindset—the belief that abilities are static rather than developed through effort—can also be a significant barrier, as individuals may view setbacks as evidence of their limitations rather than as opportunities for growth. Chronic stress, toxic environments, and negative self-perceptions further erode perseverance by fostering doubt, discouragement, and emotional exhaustion. Additionally, perfectionism can be counterproductive, as individuals who fear failure may become paralyzed by self-criticism rather than pushing forward with resilience.

Another major challenge to grit is the temptation of immediate gratification. In a world that prioritizes quick rewards, the ability to delay gratification and focus on long-term goals is increasingly rare. Traumatic adversity, while sometimes a catalyst for resilience, can also create psychological barriers to perseverance if not properly addressed. Ultimately, grit is not just about working hard—it is about cultivating a mindset that embraces setbacks, sees challenges as learning experiences, and remains committed to long-term goals despite difficulties. By developing grit, individuals build the psychological endurance necessary to achieve extraordinary success.

THE IMPORTANCE OF GRIT FOR PEAK PERFORMANCE

A crucial character strength for achieving peak performance is the ability to sustain effort, overcome obstacles, and remain steadfast through various contexts and phases of your journey. This is where grit becomes indispensable. Grit is the psychological trait that empowers individuals to maintain an unwavering focus on their goals, partnering with resilience to push beyond the initial, more enjoyable stages of goal pursuit. Those who possess grit exhibit a remarkable capacity to stay motivated and disciplined, even when immediate progress is not visible, ensuring long-term success.

While resilience is the capacity to recover and grow from adversity, grit plays a distinct yet complementary role. In any high-performance endeavor tediousness, failures, and delayed gratification are inevitable. However, individuals with grit do not see these challenges as reasons to stop but as the necessary price to achieve mastery. Instead of becoming discouraged by difficulties, they learn from them throughout the process and even view the struggle as a blessing. This perspective fuels their renewed determination, knowing that enduring these hardships will set them apart from the average. This durability ensures they remain committed to their long-term vision, regardless of external difficulties or internal doubts.

The benefits of grit extend far beyond mere goal achievement; they significantly enhance overall well-being and life satisfaction. Research indicates that grit is closely linked to higher academic and professional success, as well as improved emotional regulation and personal fulfillment. Individuals who cultivate grit are more adept at persevering through discomfort, delaying gratification, and establishing and maintaining the daily habits essential for excellence. Ultimately, grit is the driving force that allows for well-being, enabling individuals to reach their highest potential while not giving in to immediate impulses at the cost of meaningful pursuits. This steadfast commitment ensures they navigate the inevitable ups and downs of their journey with unwavering determination.[20]

EFFECTIVELY CULTIVATING AND APPLYING GRIT FOR PEAK PERFORMANCE

By deliberately cultivating grit, you can break through barriers and achieve extraordinary results. Here's how to develop and apply grit for sustained excellence and endurance for your journey to peak performance:

Step 1. Define a Purposeful Long-Term Goal

Grit thrives on purpose. To cultivate grit, start by defining a long-term goal that excites and challenges you—something truly worth pursuing, even when the journey gets tough. This goal should resonate deeply with you, igniting a passion that fuels your determination. A compelling *"why"* will anchor your commitment, providing the motivation needed to push forward when obstacles arise.

Without a strong purpose, grit cannot survive. It's essential to choose a goal that you are deeply connected to, as this connection will sustain your perseverance through the inevitable setbacks and difficulties. Reflect on what truly matters to you and identify a goal that aligns with your core values and aspirations. This meaningful connection will transform your goal into a driving force, making persistence feel less like a struggle and more like a natural part of your journey.

Remember, the strength of your purpose will correlate to the strength of your grit. By defining a meaningful long-term goal, you lay the foundation for unwavering commitment, ensuring that you stay the course even when the going gets tough.

Step 2. Develop Unshakable Discipline and a Relentless Work Ethic

Grit is about showing up—every single day. It's about putting in the work, even when you don't feel like it, and no one else cares. To cultivate grit, you must build unshakable discipline and a relentless work ethic. This means creating structured routines that keep you on track, even when motivation wanes. Embrace discomfort as a natural part of the process and commit to making small, daily improvements.

Effort sustained over time leads to mastery. The ability to push forward, regardless of circumstances, is what separates peak performers from everyone else. Developing discipline involves setting clear, achievable goals and breaking them down into manageable tasks. Establish a daily routine that prioritizes these tasks and stick to it, even when it feels tedious or difficult. Recognize that progress often comes in small increments and that each step forward, no matter how minor, contributes to your overall growth. A relentless work ethic means committing to excellence in everything you do, and pushing yourself to go the extra mile, even when it's uncomfortable or inconvenient. This dedication to continuous improvement will build your resilience and strengthen your grit, enabling you to persevere through any challenge.

Step 3. Focus on the Process, Not Just the Outcome

Success is the culmination of countless hours of planning, effort, setbacks, and refinements. Every breakthrough is built upon a foundation of learning from mistakes, adapting to challenges, and making precise adjustments along the way. If you aspire to achieve something truly significant, struggle is essential.

To cultivate grit, you must embrace the grind. This requires shifting your mindset from obsessing over the outcome to valuing the process itself. Every challenge you face is an opportunity for refinement, a chance to sharpen your skills, expand your knowledge, and develop the persistence necessary for long-term success. The greatest achievers are not those who seek instant gratification but those who persist when progress feels slow, trusting that their daily effort is laying the foundation for future breakthroughs.

Success should not be measured solely by immediate results but by steady, continuous improvement. The longer you commit to the journey without expecting instant rewards, the deeper your understanding becomes, and the more meaningful your success will be. True mastery is not a moment of triumph—it is the relentless pursuit of growth and excellence.

Step 4. Surround Yourself with Grit-Oriented Influences
Your environment has a profound impact on your ability to persist through challenges. It can either fuel your perseverance or drain your motivation. The people, places, and messages you immerse yourself in shape your mindset, influence your daily habits, and ultimately determine how persistent you remain in the face of setbacks. To cultivate grit, you must be intentional about surrounding yourself with influences that encourage persistence, growth, and a sense of purpose.

Seek out mentors, teammates, and peers who embody grit—those who push through adversity, stay disciplined in their pursuits, and refuse to give up when the journey gets difficult. Being around relentless individuals reinforces your own commitment and makes persistence feel like the norm rather than the exception, helping you internalize the belief that you, too, can overcome obstacles with unwavering determination. Beyond the people in your life, pay close attention to the messages you consume, as they can either strengthen or weaken your resolve. The books you read, the podcasts you listen to, and even the social media accounts you follow all shape your mindset. Fill your mental space with stories of perseverance, strategies for overcoming challenges, and narratives that reinforce the power of grit, ensuring that your environment consistently fuels your drive for long-term success.

Additionally, shape your physical environment to reflect your dedication to long-term success. Surround yourself with reminders of your purpose—whether it's a copy of your purpose statement, motivational quotes, or other personal items that keep you focused. Engage in purpose-driven activities that align with your values and fuel your passion. When your surroundings consistently reinforce positive emotions and meaningful pursuits, it becomes easier to stay committed, even in the face of obstacles. By surrounding yourself with those who uplift, inspire, and challenge you, you create a support system that keeps you accountable but also kindly drives you toward mastery.

Step 5. Build Self-Compassion without Making Excuses

Grit certainly does not require being overly harsh on yourself when things go wrong—it means maintaining the discipline to push forward while treating yourself with the same kindness and patience you would offer a friend. A strong commitment to your goals requires persistence, but that persistence is unsustainable without self-compassion. We must acknowledge failures as learning opportunities rather than personal flaws. Remember, as we work through difficult goal pursuits, we will not have all the answers or necessary skills. We are going to fall short frequently.

Use these struggles to refine your approach instead of allowing them to discourage you, or worse, cause you to completely disengage from the pursuit of your goals. Self-compassion enables you to recover from setbacks more effectively, preventing burnout and keeping you motivated to adjust for the long haul. However, true grit also requires accountability—being kind to yourself does not mean lowering your standards or making excuses. The key is to strike a balance: give yourself grace, but never let comfort replace progress.

Step 6. Expand Your Limits Through Challenge

Just as muscles grow through resistance, grit strengthens in the face of discomfort and challenge. Growth doesn't happen in the safety of our comfort zones—it happens when we push ourselves beyond what feels easy or familiar. To develop true grit, we must seek out progressively harder tasks, knowing that struggle is not a sign of failure but a prerequisite for growth. When we intentionally lean into difficulty, we train our minds to see discomfort not as a signal to stop but as evidence that we are learning, adapting, and improving.

Grit is certainly not about instant success; it's about doing the hard things long enough for progress to catch up. Every challenge you embrace expands your capacity for resilience, discipline, and mastery. If we cultivate grit with purpose, we will continually redefine our perceived limits, unlocking potential we could not see previously. Importantly, competence, efficacy, training, and experience all work to reduce anxiety related to new tasks. Initial struggles are a natural part of growth, but they don't have to be faced alone. Seeking mentorship, training, or support from peers can accelerate adaptation, making even the most daunting challenges manageable.

CHAPTER 7 REFLECTION: WHY GRIT IS VITAL FOR PEAK PERFORMANCE

Becoming an expert in any field and performing at your peak requires a long process of learning, failing, monitoring feedback, and adjusting. This journey demands grit to sustain us through the many challenges we will face. Only through this sustained effort can we refine our skills and grow without losing interest.

To persist with grit, we must first understand what truly drives us. Passion makes it easier to endure the difficulties that come with the commitment to mastery. However, passion alone isn't enough—our habits and daily routines must align with our goals. By consistently improving how we train, learn, and work, we shape our overall outcomes through our behaviors. Success is not a one-time event but the result of countless, consistent moments of disciplined behavior and forged habits.

Thus, grit is an indispensable ingredient of peak performance. It enables us to endure, adapt, and keep moving forward when others lose interest and abandon their dreams. If we commit to the process, stay persistent through failures, and continuously improve our approach, we will reach our goals.

Chapter 7 Action Items

- Dedicate yourself to the process, not just the results, and fine-tune your daily routines for consistent advancement. *(Time Commitment ~ 1 hour)*
- Focus on the consistency of your process rather than immediate success, and adjust to optimize its effectiveness. *(Time Commitment ~ 1 hour)*

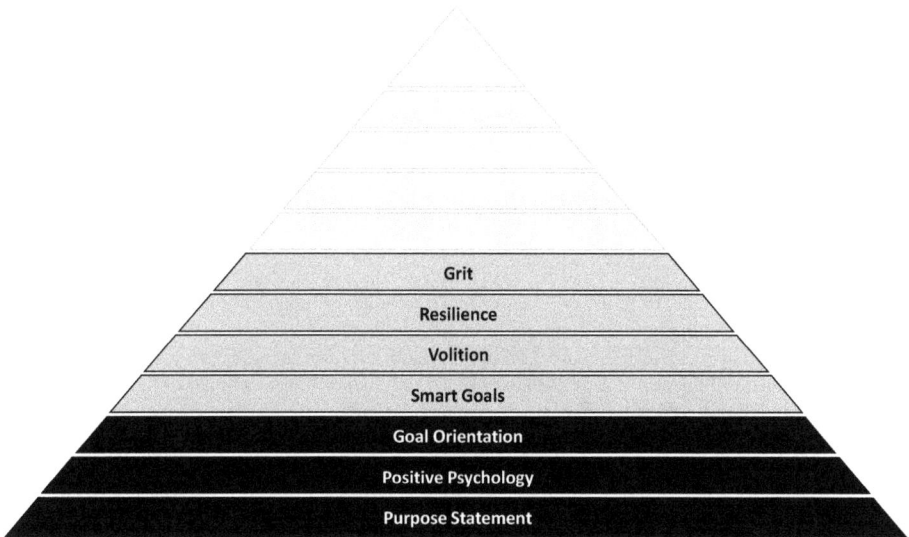

Grit

Resilience

Volition

Smart Goals

Goal Orientation

Positive Psychology

Purpose Statement

SECTION 3

THE PATH TO BECOMING EXTRAORDINARY

STORY: THE VOICE THAT DEFIED LIMITS

This section is where peak performance transforms into mastery. Up to this point, you've learned about resolve, developed foundational skills of goal pursuit, and learned how to effectively push past limitations. Now, it's time to take the next step—the step that separates the great from the truly exceptional. This final group of principles allows us to become outliers, someone whose skills are so ingrained, so automatic, that they consistently perform at a level few can ever reach. The principles ahead will show you how to make excellence second nature—where discipline and effort evolve into instinctive, world-class execution.

Mastery isn't just about working hard or showing up; it's about training with intention, aligning habits with purpose, and committing to continuous growth—even when you're already excelling. It means understanding flow state, refining skills until they become effortless, and staying on course while others falter. True masters don't just perform well—they redefine what's possible. Below is an example of someone that exemplifies the principles discussed in this section.[9, 22]

Andrea Bocelli wasn't supposed to be a world-renowned tenor. At least, that's what logic would have dictated. Born with congenital glaucoma, his vision was limited from birth, and by age 12, after a soccer accident, he was completely blind. But if blindness was supposed to be a barrier, Bocelli never saw it that way. Instead, he pursued music with an intensity that few could match.

As a child, he was fascinated by opera and classical music. He would spend hours at the piano, fully immersed in the sound, feeling every note in a way that sighted people might never appreciate. Music wasn't just a hobby—it was a sanctuary. When he played, nothing else existed. He lost himself in the rhythm and melody, entering a state of deep focus where time disappeared. It was in these moments that he first experienced what would be considered a *flow state*—that state of total immersion where performance is able to reach its peak.

But loving music wasn't enough. To become truly great, he had to refine his skill relentlessly. His passion led him to train under local teachers and later under the legendary Franco Corelli. His journey was not easy. He worked as a lawyer by day and played piano in bars by night, constantly honing his voice. Every hour spent singing, every correction from a mentor, and every repetition of a phrase brought him one step closer to mastery. His training wasn't just about practice—it was about *deliberate* practice. He dissected performances, studied the greats, and continuously refined his vocal technique.

As he dedicated himself fully to his craft, excellence became second nature. What once required intense focus—breathing techniques, phrasing, emotional delivery—became automatic. His muscle memory and vocal control allowed him to perform with ease, freeing his mind to focus on interpretation rather than mechanics. He had reached a level where skill and habit merged, where his years of training allowed him to step onto a stage and deliver a flawless performance without overthinking every note.

But skill alone isn't enough to reach outlier status. Much of Bocelli's success came from aligning his goals with his actions. Despite pressure to pursue a stable career in law, he remained unwavering in his pursuit of music. Every choice he made, from his training to his lifestyle, propelled him toward his ultimate vision. When a demo tape of him singing found its way to Italian pop star Zucchero, and then to the great Luciano Pavarotti, Bocelli's preparation had made him ready for this occasion. He stepped up and performed with confidence—not just because he had talent, but because every moment of his life had been preparing him for that opportunity.

Today, Bocelli is not just a singer—he is a phenomenon. With over 90 million records sold, he is one of the best-selling classical artists of all time. His ability to blend classical opera with contemporary music has set him apart, making opera accessible to the world. His journey wasn't about luck. It was about deep focus, skill refinement, goal-congruent habits, and a relentless pursuit of greatness. Bocelli's story shows that our performance is built by fully immersing in our craft, refining our skills, automating success habits, aligning our behaviors and resources with our goals, and pushing beyond our limits.

In these final chapters, we'll begin with flow state—the key to unlocking peak performance on demand. From there, we'll explore lifelong skill development, not as mere hard work, but as a deliberate and strategic path to mastery that ensures continued growth long after others would plateau.

Next, we'll uncover how to hardwire success through automaticity, turning elite execution into second nature. We will then examine goal-congruent behavior, eliminating distractions and pseudo-effort so that every action drives real progress. Finally, we'll define what it means to be an outlier.

Mastery isn't about being better than average—it's about breaking past self-imposed limits and continuously elevating your performance past what was once impossible. While others settle for adequacy, you'll be accelerating toward greatness. These final chapters explain the psychology needed for sustaining elite performance while protecting your mental and physical well-being. It's time to push beyond your current limits and step fully into an extraordinary life. Let's begin.

CHAPTER 8

FLOW STATE

TAPPING INTO PEAK PERFORMANCE FLOW

STORY: MASTERING THE FLOW STATE

It's midnight, but Tony Robbins shows no signs of slowing down. He's been on stage for over ten hours, pacing with boundless energy, engaging with thousands in the crowd as if he were speaking to each person individually. His voice booms with conviction, his movements are electric, and his mind is razor-sharp. He remembers names, details, and even emotions shared by audience members hours earlier. Despite the intensity of his performance, he looks just as energized as when he began. This isn't just passion—it's *flow*.

Tony Robbins has built an empire by mastering the ability to fully immerse himself in the present moment. His seminars last for twelve to sixteen hours straight, yet he never loses focus or enthusiasm. He enters a state of complete engagement, where time seems to slow down, distractions disappear, and his energy flows effortlessly. His ability to sustain such an extraordinary level of performance is both a skill and a science.

From an early age, Robbins sought to understand what makes people excel. He immersed himself in psychology, neurolinguistic programming, and human behavior, studying the habits of top performers. He trained his mind and body to operate at an elite level, conditioning himself to enter a flow state on command. Whether speaking to a stadium of 15,000 people, coaching world leaders, or writing bestsellers, he taps into a level of focus and immersion that allows him to perform at an extraordinary level.

This is more than just about passion—Robbins has trained himself to trigger flow through specific rituals. Before every event, he primes his mind and body with a series of deliberate actions: ice baths to shock his system, intense breathing exercises to flood his body with oxygen, and powerful movements to channel his energy. These aren't random habits; they are precise mechanisms to ensure that when he steps on stage, he enters a state of complete immersion.

What makes Robbins an outlier is his ability to combine his knowledge perfectly with his task, resulting in consistent peak performance. His mastery of flow allows him to achieve what most people would consider impossible: delivering marathon-length seminars with unbreakable focus, making instant and profound connections with individuals, and maintaining unstoppable momentum that has propelled him to the top of his field.

Tony Robbins doesn't just use flow—he *lives* in it. His story proves that when you learn to enter this state at will, your ability to achieve extraordinary results becomes limitless.

Definition of Flow State

Flow state refers to a mental state in which an individual is fully immersed in an activity, experiencing a sense of energized focus, full involvement, and enjoyment in the process. This state is often described as being "in the zone," where time seems to fly by, and the person feels a deep sense of involvement and accomplishment. Flow occurs when there is a perfect balance between the difficulty of the task at hand and the individual's skill level, creating an optimal environment for peak performance.

Achieving a flow state is closely linked to peak performance, as it allows individuals to perform at their highest potential. When in flow, people experience heightened creativity, improved problem-solving abilities, and increased productivity. Athletes, artists, and professionals across various fields often report their best work occurring during these moments of deep immersion. The key to reaching this state lies in finding tasks that are neither too easy nor too difficult, providing just the right amount of challenge to keep the individual engaged and passionate.

Several triggers are critical for achieving a flow state. Clear goals and immediate feedback are essential, as they help individuals stay passionate and focused while adjusting their actions in real-time. Additionally, eliminating distractions and creating an environment conducive to concentration can significantly enhance the likelihood of entering flow. Strengthening your skills is equally vital—continuously refining your PERMA elements, VIA strengths, and unique talents allows you to unlock your full potential. By building on what you excel at, you can make meaningful breakthroughs with your efforts.[7]

When challenges arise, the ability to operate at your very best becomes crucial, and a well-developed skillset enables you to meet obstacles with confidence. Relatedly, physical and mental preparation, such as practicing emotional awareness, regular exercise, and a maintained healthy lifestyle, also play a crucial role in facilitating this state. By understanding and leveraging these triggers, individuals can more consistently tap into the power of flow, unlocking their potential for extraordinary performance.

The Importance of Flow for Peak Performance

Peak performance requires working with your best effort along with total engagement, clarity, and purpose. When you enter a flow state, you unlock your ability to perform at your highest level, effortlessly balancing challenge and skill while fully immersed in the task at hand. This state of deep focus allows you to push past limitations, harnessing your strengths with precision and efficiency.

Flow is characterized by intense concentration, clear goals, and immediate feedback, creating a seamless connection between effort and outcome. To reach this state, you must align three critical elements: your *purpose*, your *skills*, and your *environment*. When these factors are in harmony, work becomes intrinsically rewarding, and productivity soars. Rather than chasing effort, you direct your energy toward meaningful and effective results.[27]

Your path to flourishing will naturally align with your purpose, as operating in flow requires harmony with both your passion and purpose. This allows you to invest aggressively in your development resulting in long-term fulfillment without the regret of wasted time or resources. By aligning your purpose, refining your strengths, and shaping your environment, you create a life where obstacles seem both worthwhile and manageable. Additionally, the excitement of pursuing your purpose will provide fuel for your growth. This approach ensures that your peak performance is not an occasional achievement but a consistent expectation.

Undoubtedly, your strengths must also be leveraged to unlock sustained excellence. By recognizing and refining your unique abilities—whether through the VIA test or self-reflection—you ensure that your efforts align with your core values. This alignment not only enhances performance but also fosters intrinsic motivation, grit, and resilience, allowing you to navigate life's challenges with both passion and confidence. A deep understanding of your skills enables you to apply them across all areas of life—work, relationships, and personal growth—maximizing your ability to perform under pressure.[28]

Finally, achieving peak performance also requires creating an intentional workspace. Distractions are the enemy of deep focus, and minimizing them is essential to sustaining engagement. Optimizing your surroundings for comfort and efficiency—whether by eliminating clutter, controlling noise levels, or structuring your time effectively—sets the stage for uninterrupted immersion. A well-designed workspace doesn't just improve productivity; it creates the conditions necessary for flow to occur naturally and consistently.

EFFECTIVELY ACHIEVING THE FLOW STATE FOR PEAK PERFORMANCE

Achieving flow is a deliberate process that requires aligning your focus, skills, and environment to reach peak performance. This requires intense focus, clear goals, a balance between the difficulty of the task and one's skills, and intense, intrinsic interest in the task. While in flow, you will achieve peak performance and maximize the effectiveness of your strengths and skills. By following the steps below, you will increase your ability to tap into the flow state to maximize your performance:

Step 1: Set Clear Goals with Immediate Feedback

Flow thrives on clarity, passion, and intrinsic motivation. We should define specific, achievable goals that align with our purpose statement while also challenging us without over-whelming us. Our objectives need to be well-defined so that we always know exactly what we are trying to accomplish. Pairing this with immediate feedback—whether from self-assessment, a mentor, or real-time results—will allow us to make quick adjustments and maintain momentum.

Additionally, flow is most easily sustained when the task itself is rewarding. Align your work with your passions, strengths, and values to fuel intrinsic motivation. When we find deep satisfaction in what we're doing, the flow state becomes a natural outcome rather than something we must force.

Step 2: Match Challenge with Skill Level

Achieving flow requires a perfect balance between the difficulty of a task and your abilities. Thus, continuously improving and refining your skills is essential to maintain this balance. You must avoid complacency when your skills are merely adequate to perform your tasks; instead, strive to push slightly beyond your comfort zone to create continuous growth.

Finding the optimal level of challenge is crucial for full engagement. If a task is too easy, we will only utilize a small fraction of our potential. Conversely, if it's too difficult, we may experience anxiety or disengage to protect our self-esteem. Aim for a challenge that stretches your abilities just enough to keep you fully immersed and motivated.

Step 3: Eliminate Distractions and Create an Immersive Environment

Creating the right environment and mindset is crucial for achieving and sustaining deep focus. Start by eliminating distractions: silence notifications, organize your physical space, and set boundaries with others to minimize interruptions.

Design a workspace that promotes concentration and immersion.

Next, establish a pre-flow ritual to signal to your brain that it's time to enter flow. This could include mindfulness exercises, deep breathing, aromatherapy, or reviewing your goals. A consistent pre-flow routine helps condition your mind and body to transition smoothly into a highly focused state.

Finally, fully immerse yourself in the task at hand. Commit to the present moment, avoiding multitasking or letting your mind wander. Flow is most powerful when you are completely absorbed in your work, losing track of time and feeling fully in sync with your actions.

Step 4: Develop Clarity and Stamina for the Flow State through Consistency

Achieving flow becomes easier with regular practice, much like mastering any other skill. By consistently engaging in focused, challenging work, we strengthen our ability to enter and sustain this state. Over time, this practice expands our capacity for deep work, transforming peak performance into a sustainable habit. While developing this stamina requires dedication and persistence, the rewards—enhanced productivity, fulfillment, and a greater sense of accomplishment—make the effort well worthwhile.

Moreover, by intentionally following these steps, we gain a clearer understanding of how to enter flow and extend its duration. Naturally, this process involves periods of struggle as we refine our ability to tap into deep focus. However, each attempt teaches us valuable lessons, allowing us to improve with time. As we cultivate our flow state more effectively, we experience extraordinary productivity, deeper engagement, and consistently high performance. Even if it takes years of deliberate practice, the long-term benefits are undeniable. Once this process takes hold, our productivity soars, and operating at our peak becomes second nature—proving that the investment of time and effort is more than worth it.

CHAPTER 8 REFLECTION: HOW FLOW UNLOCKS PEAK PERFORMANCE

Achieving flow is essential for lasting well-being, significantly enhancing your ability to accomplish meaningful work and make a lasting impact. By aligning your purpose, refining your strengths, optimizing your environment, and intentionally practicing flow, you create the conditions for deep engagement and sustained success. Flow empowers you to maximize your time, rise to challenges, and unlock your full potential.

With a clear purpose guiding your path, a commitment to continuous skill development, and a habit of refining your workspace while minimizing distractions, your ability to enter and sustain flow will continually improve. This mastery will not only set you apart from your peers but also enable you to achieve peak performance with remarkable consistency. As a result, you will amplify your impact, cultivate a personal brand synonymous with excellence, and learn to harness flow to elevate all aspects of your life and overall well-being.

CHAPTER 8 ACTION ITEMS

• Arrange and optimize your work area to remove distractions and ready your mind for deep focus. *(Time Commitment ~ 2 hours)*

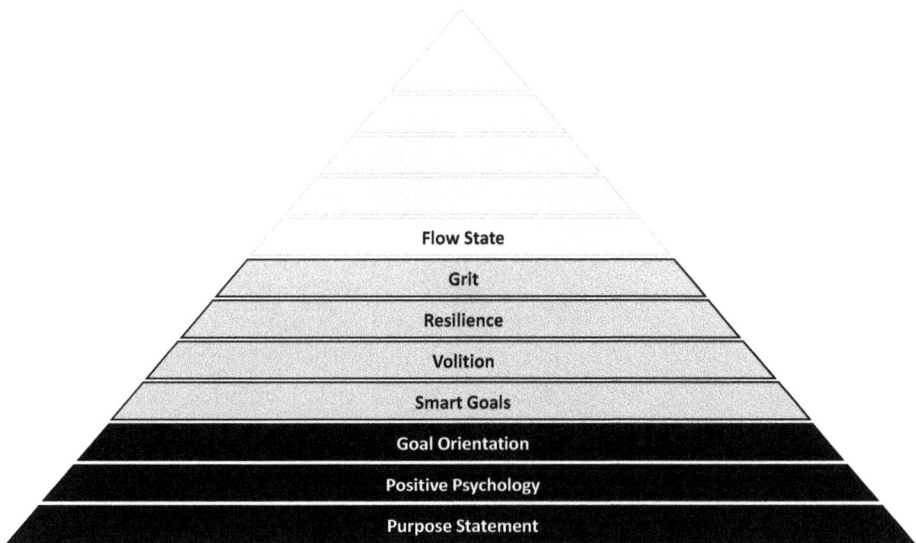

CHAPTER 9
SKILL DEVELOPMENT
CULTIVATING SKILLS TO FUEL EXTRAORDINARY SUCCESS

STORY: FROM STRUGGLE TO MASTER SURGEON

As a child growing up in poverty in Detroit, Ben Carson faced seemingly insurmountable challenges. Raised by a single mother with only a third-grade education, he struggled academically and was often mocked by classmates for his poor performance. By the time he was in fifth grade, Carson was at the bottom of his class, believing he wasn't smart enough to succeed. But his mother, Sonya Carson, refused to let him accept mediocrity. She imposed a strict rule: instead of watching television for hours, he and his brother had to read two books a week and write reports—even though she couldn't read the reports herself to check them.

At first, Carson resented this new routine. Reading was difficult, and improving his skills felt overwhelming. But as he persisted, something extraordinary happened—his mind sharpened, his curiosity deepened, and he discovered a love for learning. He went from failing grades to excelling in school, proving that intelligence wasn't fixed but something that could be cultivated through deliberate practice and discipline.

Carson's transformation didn't stop with academics. His dream of becoming a doctor pushed him to continuously level up his abilities, leading him to Yale University and eventually to Johns Hopkins Medical School. But his greatest challenge—and defining moment—came when he entered the field of pediatric neurosurgery.

As a young surgeon, Carson understood that technical skills, decision-making under pressure, and relentless preparation would determine his success. He honed his expertise through thousands of hours of practice, refining his precision, improving his speed, and studying the most complex brain surgeries in history. His commitment to mastery led to one of the most extraordinary surgical breakthroughs of all time—the successful separation of conjoined twins, Patrick and Benjamin Binder, in 1987. The 22-hour procedure required an unprecedented level of skill, teamwork, and problem-solving—all built on years of relentless improvement.

Ben Carson's story proves that mastery isn't about natural talent—it's about commitment to growth. He went from being labeled an underperformer to pioneering life-saving surgeries because he embraced deliberate learning, practiced with intention, and never stopped improving. His journey shows us that no matter where we start, extraordinary success is possible when we dedicate ourselves to skill growth, resilience, and lifelong learning.

DEFINITION OF SKILL DEVELOPMENT

Skill growth is the continuous process of improving one's abilities through deliberate practice, targeted learning, and flexible problem-solving. It is a fundamental aspect of human development and performance enhancement, involving the expansion of both cognitive and motor skills over time. Psychologically, skill growth is driven by neuroplasticity, the brain's ability to rewire itself through repeated effort and experience. It is also influenced by self-efficacy—the confidence in one's abilities—and growth mindset, the conviction that abilities can be developed rather than being fixed traits.[19]

Skill growth occurs through deliberate practice, a structured method of training that pushes an individual slightly beyond their current capabilities, creating an optimal level of challenge. Research by Anders Ericsson on expertise development suggests that mastery is achieved not merely by repetition, but by purposeful, feedback-driven engagement. As individuals push their limits, their neural pathways strengthen, leading to improved efficiency and automaticity in performance. [29]

Additionally, self-regulated learning plays a crucial role, as those who actively reflect on their progress, set challenging goals, avoid distractions, and adjust their strategies experience accelerated improvement. Incorporating skill growth into daily life requires intentional learning and resilience in the face of setbacks. Whether in academics, sports, business, or creative fields, those who embrace failure as feedback and persist in refining their abilities can achieve extraordinary success. Furthermore, skill stacking—the combination of multiple competencies—enhances versatility and innovation, setting high achievers apart. By continuously improving one's skills and applying them to meaningful pursuits, individuals not only reach peak performance but also gain a deep sense of fulfillment and purpose in their work.

THE IMPORTANCE OF SKILL DEVELOPMENT FOR PEAK PERFORMANCE

Achieving peak performance will always be reliant on continuous skill development through deliberate practice. Research by K. Anders Ericsson and Neil Charness (1994) emphasizes that expert performance is built through sustained, structured training rather than innate ability. Their study highlights that those who reach elite levels in any field—whether in music, athletics, medicine, or business—do so through systematic efforts to refine their skills over years of dedicated practice. This process requires not just repetition, but focused engagement, immediate feedback, and incremental challenges that push the individual beyond their current level of competence.[19] Without this deliberate effort to grow, performance will plateau, and the potential for extraordinary performance will never be realized.[29]

A critical psychological benefit produced with skill growth is self-efficacy. Ericsson and Charness's research indicate that individuals who trust in their capacity to develop expertise are more likely to persist through setbacks, engage in more challenging learning experiences, and refine their techniques over time. As skills improve, self-efficacy strengthens, creating a positive feedback loop—the more one succeeds, the more confidence one gains, fueling greater motivation to continue refining their abilities. This cycle certainly distinguishes top performers from the average as the internalization of progress creates a foundation for ever-greater achievements.

Furthermore, deliberate practice restructures cognitive and motor processes, making tasks that once required significant effort to become more efficient and automatic. This offers evidence that peak performers leverage mental representations—highly developed internal models of their craft—to make faster, more precise decisions. This allows them to function at an elite level under high-pressure conditions, demonstrating expertise that appears effortless but is actually the product of thousands of hours of purposeful training and refinement. When individuals commit to ongoing skill development, they unlock their full potential for peak performance, setting themselves apart as outliers in their respective fields.

EFFECTIVE SKILL DEVELOPMENT FOR PEAK PERFORMANCE

Developing your strengths and skills is a crucial key to operating at your absolute best. By continually building your capabilities, you prepare yourself for future challenges and opportunities. Importantly, with each step forward, your confidence will also grow, and you will experience less anxiety and greater joy in your work. This alignment between skill development and task engagement will fuel intrinsic motivation, making the journey along your life's purpose profoundly rewarding.

During the process, consistent growth of your competency will help you establish a foundation of expertise. By consistently pushing your boundaries despite already meeting minimum standards, you will ensure improved performance over time. By focusing on consistent growth, you position yourself for extraordinary success, setting a solid reputation that fuels motivation and allows you to operate at peak performance.

To cultivate skill development as a habit and reach peak performance, follow these key steps:

Step 1: Identify Your Core Strengths and Growth Areas

Begin by assessing your natural talents and current skill level. Tools like the VIA Character Strengths Survey or reviewing professional skill requirements for your organization can help identify areas where you excel and those that require focus and improvement. Reflecting on past successes and challenges provides valuable insights into your strengths and areas for required growth. This self-awareness acts as a roadmap, guiding you toward targeted skill development that will elevate your performance and help you achieve focused mastery.

Keep in mind that when life is at its worst or when pressure from responsibilities intensifies, we must be at our best. To prepare for these moments, we must continuously refine even our strongest skills, ensuring they remain sharp and adaptable. Growth is not only about addressing weaknesses but also about deepening expertise and expanding capabilities. Additionally, we may need to recognize shortcomings that could hinder progress and take proactive steps to either improve or mitigate them through training, strategic learning, or environmental adjustments. By committing to ongoing development, we fortify ourselves against adversity, enabling us to rise to the occasion with confidence and competence.

Step 2: Set Clear, Targeted Milestones

Once you've identified your strengths and areas for improvement, establish SMART goals that align with your long-term ambitions. These target milestones create structure and accountability, ensuring that your practice remains purposeful and consistent rather than random. Setting incremental targets also makes growth manageable and motivating, reinforcing progress along the way.[22]

For example, if your goal is to improve leadership skills, you might establish several intermediate milestones to ensure steady development. First, you could complete a leadership training course within the next three months to build foundational knowledge. Next, you might set a goal to actively complete LinkedIn training for six months, providing structured progress to areas of interest. To improve communication and presence, you could aim to deliver at least one public speech or presentation per quarter, gradually increasing in complexity and audience size. Additionally, setting a milestone to read and summarize one leadership book per month would enhance strategic thinking and decision-making skills. By consistently progressing through these structured steps, you build confidence, competence, and credibility, ultimately positioning yourself for greater leadership effectiveness and long-term success.

Step 3: Engage in Deliberate Training and Practice

Skill development requires deliberate practice, meaning highly focused, structured efforts aimed at improvement. Rather than just repeating a task, deliberate practice involves breaking down complex skills, seeking expert feedback, and refining performance through constant adjustment. This approach helps you push beyond your current limitations and develop expertise efficiently.

One way to engage in deliberate practice is to actively seek out opportunities that challenge you while aligning with your long-term growth goals. For instance, volunteering to assist your boss on projects outside your regular responsibilities can provide hands-on experience in areas you want to improve. If leadership and communication are skills you wish to develop, you might offer to prepare presentations or lead team meetings to strengthen your public speaking and strategic thinking.

If you're interested in process improvement, consider investigating inefficiencies within your organization and proposing a structured initiative to enhance productivity. Additionally, assisting with high-visibility projects can expose you to new challenges, decision-making processes, and valuable mentorship from senior leaders. By intentionally seeking out growth-focused opportunities, you create an environment where consistent learning, adaptation, and mastery become a natural part of your development journey.

Step 4: Consistently Optimize Your Environment for Growth

Sustaining peak performance requires a structured environment, consistent habits, and a mindset that embraces challenge and adaptation. Competency provides a foundation, but consistency turns growth into mastery. Establish daily or weekly routines that reinforce skill development—whether by dedicating focused practice time, reviewing past work for improvements, or tracking progress. Over time, these habits compound, driving continuous advancement.

Growth also demands stepping beyond your comfort zone. Engage in challenges that stretch your abilities while remaining within a productive difficulty range to avoid frustration. Adaptability in the face of obstacles fosters resilience and strengthens your capacity to perform under pressure—a key trait of peak performers. Additionally, your environment plays a critical role in skill development. Minimize distractions, create a workspace that encourages deep focus, and surround yourself with mentors and high-achievers who inspire growth. A well-optimized setting enhances learning, making deliberate practice more effective.

Finally, regular reflection and refinement ensure sustained progress. Track key metrics, keep a performance log to document progress, and regularly analyze both achievements and setbacks. By celebrating small wins and adjusting your strategies based on insights gained, you reinforce motivation and maintain momentum toward mastery. Be prepared for some negative feedback, as pushing our performance boundaries often means starting below average. When skill development becomes a deliberate, structured, and consistent practice, success follows naturally—allowing you to operate at your highest level and achieve extraordinary results.

Chapter 9 Reflection: Using Skill Development to Generate Peak Performance

Peak performance is the result of thousands of hours of deliberate practice, refinement, and continuous learning. No one becomes extraordinary without first mastering the ordinary. Every expert, no matter how talented, has endured the struggle of being a beginner and failing repeatedly before reaching excellence. This process of growth is neither quick nor easy, but it is essential.

Failure, while often discouraging, is not a sign of ineptness—it is a necessary part of skill development. We must fail, adjust, and fail again before we break through to mastery. Seeking out and embracing negative feedback can feel like a threat to our ego, but without honest and accurate assessments, improvement stalls. The most successful individuals do not avoid criticism; they actively pursue mentorship and guidance, using feedback as a tool to refine their skills and strategies. Growth demands that we push past comfort, willingly exposing ourselves to difficulties that stretch our abilities while being careful not to become overwhelmed.

Equally important, we must never allow our strengths to plateau. The moment we assume we have "arrived" is the moment progress halts. Just as an athlete continues training even after reaching peak form, we must keep sharpening our abilities, reinforcing and expanding what we do well while mitigating weaknesses that could limit our success. This requires discipline, consistency, and the formation of habits that prioritize skill development. Without this ongoing refinement, peak performance remains an unattainable ideal rather than a lived reality. By committing to lifelong growth, we lay the foundation for sustained excellence, turning potential into achievement and struggle into extraordinary success.

CHAPTER 9 ACTION ITEMS

- Choose skill training that amplifies your strengths and sign up now. *(Time Commitment ~ 1 hour)*
- Create a work environment and weekly routine that prioritize skill development. *(Time Commitment ~ 1 hour)*

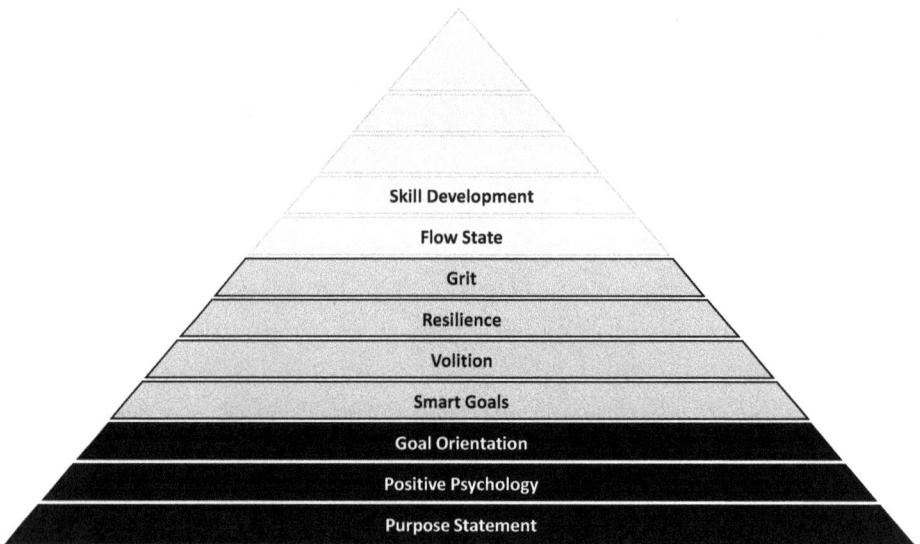

CHAPTER 10

AUTOMATICITY

AUTOMATING SUCCESS FOR PEAK PERFORMANCE

STORY: THE INCREDIBLE POWER OF DAILY HABITS

A compelling example of automating extraordinary success is Benjamin Franklin—a self-made virtuoso who dedicated his life to skill improvement and lifelong learning, transforming himself from a humble apprentice into one of history's most influential figures. Born into a modest family, Franklin had limited formal education, yet he became a renowned writer, inventor, scientist, statesman, and philosopher. His mastery was the result of deliberate practice, insatiable curiosity, and relentless self-improvement.

As a young man, he recognized that to achieve success, he needed to constantly improve his skills. He began by methodically improving his writing, analyzing well-crafted essays, and rewriting them from memory to sharpen his communication. Through this disciplined practice, he became a persuasive writer, a skill that later helped him influence political movements and shape the founding principles of the United States.

Franklin's commitment to self-improvement extended beyond writing. He established a rigorous daily routine designed to maximize productivity, setting clear goals and reflecting on his progress each evening. He created the Junto, a group of intellectuals who challenged each other to grow and learn, and he practiced his famous 13 Virtues, a personal system for character development. These deliberate habits allowed him to continually refine his abilities, leading to groundbreaking scientific discoveries, diplomatic successes, and lasting contributions to society.

Franklin's extraordinary success shows the level of success that can be achieved by those who commit to habitual skill development. His journey proves that by habitually sharpening our strengths, practicing deliberately, and embracing lifelong learning, we can not only achieve personal mastery but also make a profound impact on the world.

By embedding productive routines into his daily life, his habits and repeated actions streamlined his effort and enhanced his efficiency. Franklin was able to operate on autopilot, freeing up mental resources for creative and strategic thinking. One of the key benefits of automaticity is that it reduces the cognitive load required to perform tasks. When actions become habitual, they require less conscious thought, allowing individuals to focus on more complex and demanding activities. Franklin's disciplined approach to writing, for example, became second nature, enabling him to produce influential works with ease.

Moreover, automaticity fosters consistency and reliability. Franklin's adherence to his daily routine and his practice of the 13 Virtues ensured that he consistently worked toward his goals, regardless of external circumstances. This unwavering commitment to his habits allowed him to make steady progress and achieve remarkable success over time.

In essence, Franklin's life illustrates how automaticity can be harnessed to build powerful habits that drive success. By automating routine tasks and embedding productive behaviors into our daily lives, we can enhance our efficiency, achieve peak performance, and ultimately, create success without requiring impossible levels of will-power.

DEFINITION OF AUTOMATICITY

Automaticity is the ability to perform tasks effortlessly and efficiently due to repeated practice, allowing actions to occur with minimal conscious effort. In psychology, this construct refers to the process by which behaviors, once effortful and intentional, become ingrained as habits—freeing up cognitive resources for more complex decision-making. When a skill or behavior reaches automaticity, it feels natural, almost second nature, requiring little to no active thought.

This phenomenon is what enables elite athletes to react instinctively in high-pressure moments, musicians to play intricate pieces without thinking about each note, and top-performing professionals to execute complex tasks with ease. The key to developing automaticity lies in consistent, deliberate repetition. When an action is repeated under the same conditions, neural pathways strengthen, making the behavior more efficient over time. Eventually, what once required effort becomes as seamless as tying a shoe or navigating a familiar route home.

The power of automaticity is that it transforms self-improvement from a struggle into a system. Instead of relying on motivation or willpower—both of which fluctuate—automatic behaviors ensure consistency. Once a productive habit is embedded, it eliminates the daily decision-making battle. There's no debate about whether to train, study, or practice; you simply do it because it has become a part of who you are. This is why the world's highest achievers don't just work hard occasionally—they automate excellence through structured routines and habits.

By intentionally shaping automatic behaviors, we can turn even the most challenging skills into effortless actions. The key is to choose the right habits to cultivate, because, just as good habits can propel us toward success, unproductive habits can work against us. Automaticity is not just about efficiency—it's about purposefully engineering a lifestyle that supports peak performance, making success feel natural.

THE IMPORTANCE OF AUTOMATICITY FOR PEAK PERFORMANCE

Achieving peak performance certainly requires discipline and effort. However, while willpower plays a role in initiating our performance preparation, it is a finite resource that depletes over time, especially under stress, fatigue, or cognitive overload. Relying solely on our willpower to sustain high levels of achievement is an unsustainable strategy. This is why top performers do not depend on limited bursts of discipline; instead, they establish automatic habits that ensure consistency regardless of external circumstances. This automaticity allows individuals to maintain peak performance without the constant mental strain of decision-making.

Habits, once ingrained, become the foundation for long-term success. Through repeated practice and reinforcement, behaviors that once required deliberate effort become almost effortless. This process streamlines actions, conserves mental energy, and allows for greater focus on more complex tasks. For example, an athlete does not consciously think about their running form during a race, nor does a skilled musician focus on every finger placement during a performance. Their years of practice have automated these movements, freeing their minds for strategic thinking and adaptation in real-time.

Beyond efficiency, automaticity fosters behavioral consistency. Inconsistent efforts produce inconsistent results, making it difficult to build momentum toward success. However, when positive habits are embedded into daily routines, they create a stable framework that supports growth. Whether it is a writer who commits to drafting a set number of words each morning or a leader who engages in online training every evening, the key to mastery is sustained, structured practice. Over time, these small, automated actions accumulate into significant achievements.

Additionally, habits simplify decision-making by reducing cognitive friction. When an action becomes automatic, it removes the internal debate of whether or not to engage in a behavior. There is no need to decide each day whether to exercise, practice a skill, or engage in productive work— these actions happen as naturally as brushing one's teeth. This eliminates the drain on mental resources and ensures that essential tasks are completed regardless of motivation levels. By intentionally shaping and reinforcing the right habits, individuals create an environment where success is just a matter of time.

Automaticity is the key to maintaining excellence without exhausting willpower. It transforms self-discipline from an act of constant struggle into a seamless process that operates in the background of daily life. Those who harness the power of automaticity do not just reach peak performance; they sustain it effortlessly, allowing them to focus on innovation, creativity, and long-term success.[30]

EFFECTIVELY DEVELOPING AUTOMATICITY FOR PEAK PERFORMANCE

Creating automatic, habitual behavior is the key to sustaining peak performance without exhausting willpower. While motivation and discipline can help initiate change, they are unreliable for long-term success. Automaticity transforms essential behaviors into effortless routines, allowing individuals to perform at a high level with minimal mental strain. This process requires intentional design, consistency, and reinforcement to ensure that habits align with long-term goals. By following a structured approach, automaticity can be cultivated in a way that enhances efficiency, focus, and sustained excellence.

Step 1. Identify where Willpower is Failing

Recognize the specific areas where self-discipline alone is insufficient to maintain progress. Willpower is a limited resource that diminishes and is unreliable. Since peak performance requires consistent growth, it is essential to pinpoint the behaviors that are critical to your goals but which you are prone to neglect. Take note of instances where motivation wavers or where maintaining consistency feels like a struggle. These moments highlight opportunities to replace reliance on willpower with structured habits that require less conscious effort

Step 2. Identify Goal-Congruent Behaviors

Once you've identified your weak points, it's crucial to clearly define behaviors that align with your long-term goals. These behaviors should be both achievable and directly tied to success. For example, if a high school student's goal is to become an engineer, a goal-congruent behavior would be committing to daily math practice along with additional math courses rather than sporadic study sessions. By ensuring that your behaviors directly support your objectives, you can eventually harness the power of automaticity to make consistent progress once it is fully established.

As you start to insert these goal-congruent behaviors into your daily routine, begin with simple, manageable actions that you are confident with and that can be performed consistently. These behaviors should be both achievable and directly tied to your desired long-term success. From our above example, if your goal is to become an engineer, begin with a single extra problem per day that can be easily integrated into your daily routine. Over time, increase the habit's intensity or frequency, allowing it to solidify into an automatic process without creating resistance. Understand that habits must be built gradually to become sustainable.

Step 3. Create Triggers for Habits

Triggers are indispensable for embedding habits into our daily life. A trigger is any cue that initiates a behavior automatically, such as bedtime triggering brushing our teeth, or arriving at work and having a cup of coffee. By linking new habits to existing routines or environmental cues, the brain learns to associate the trigger with the action, reducing the need for conscious effort.

These triggers should be clear and encountered consistently each day. Using work-day cues has been revealed through research as being useful for habit formation. This familiarity in routine allows for stability and predictability vital for cue development and habit formation. It is, however, important to keep in mind that variation created by weekends and vacations can interrupt our goal-congruent habits and cause us to revert back to old behaviors.[32] This points to the further usefulness of using cues with a large range of settings. Cues with a broad range of exposure such as waking up, going to bed, or eating a meal provide utility for our desired behavioral actions.

Some good examples of inserting new behaviors through cues might be waking up and immediately putting on workout clothes to exercise or using meal time as a cue to prompt you to complete a section of an online training course. As you insert these new behaviors and trigger cues, remember that they must be enjoyable to us. Additionally, the cues that are useful to us will assist in consistent encounters. It takes between 18 and 256 days to establish a new behavior, so patience and commitment will be very important initially as we begin to harness the cue. [33]

Step 4. Reinforce with Positive Feedback

Reinforcement strengthens the habit loop and ensures long-term adherence. Acknowledge small wins by tracking progress, celebrating milestones, or associating habits with enjoyable rewards. For example, if your new habit is completing an online certification, celebrate completing sections of that course as well as the number of associated tasks you completed at the end of each week to create a sense of achievement. Positive reinforcement encourages repetition, making the habit more ingrained over time. Goal-congruent behaviors will not become habits quickly. Thus, it is important to understand that positive reinforcement, whether through self-recognition, tracking progress, or external rewards, enhances motivation and encourages habit retention.

Step 5. Adapt and Iterate

Developing automaticity is not a static process. As life contexts change, habits must evolve to remain effective. Regularly assess whether your routines are still serving your goals and adjust them as needed. If a habit becomes stale, difficult to maintain, or ineffective at growing your skills, modify the trigger, timing, or behavior to maintain effective engagement. Don't abandon your progress out of frustration. Remember the value of failure, grit, and resilience to your long-term success. Thus, flexibility must be part of the habit-forming process to ensure your habits remain useful and aligned with your long-term objectives. Continuous refinement ensures that automaticity remains an asset in your pursuit of peak performance.[31]

By purposefully and systematically developing automaticity, we can shift from relying on our willpower and lumbering toward our goals to leveraging deeply ingrained habits that drive us consistently toward extraordinary success. This structured approach eliminates indecisiveness, enhances efficiency, and allows for sustained peak performance with minimal effort.

CHAPTER 10 REFLECTION: HOW AUTOMATICITY UNLEASHES PEAK PERFORMANCE

Automaticity is the key to sustaining peak performance without the constant drain of willpower. Throughout this chapter, we explored how habits transform goal-oriented behaviors into effortless routines, reducing cognitive strain and allowing for consistent excellence. By engineering an environment that reinforces productive habits, we replace the unpredictability of motivation with a structured system that supports success. While discipline is required to establish automaticity, the long-term reward is a streamlined, high-efficiency approach to achieving our goals.

One of the most powerful advantages of automaticity is its ability to eliminate our reliance on willpower. Since willpower is a finite resource that depletes with decision fatigue, stress, and distractions, it is not a sustainable strategy for long-term success. Automatic habits, however, bypass this limitation by embedding desired behaviors into daily life. Once a habit is ingrained, it functions without conscious effort, ensuring that goal-congruent actions occur consistently, even when motivation is low.

Automaticity also allows us to perform under pressure. When habits become deeply ingrained, they create a default mode of excellence that is resistant to external stressors. Whether an athlete competing in high-stakes events or a professional navigating demanding projects, automaticity ensures that performance remains steady regardless of external conditions. This ability to rely on well-established behaviors minimizes hesitation, enhances efficiency, and fosters a state of flow where peak performance becomes second nature. [31]

Finally, automaticity eliminates the fluctuations of motivation that often derail progress. Motivation is inherently unstable, rising and falling due to emotional states, external influences, and unforeseen obstacles. By replacing motivation with structured habits, we remove the guesswork from success. Excellence can be automated through an engineered lifestyle that leverages cues to trigger goal-congruent behaviors. The initial effort to create habits is an investment that soon yields exponential returns, allowing individuals to sustain high performance without mental exhaustion.

Ultimately, automaticity is the bridge between intention and achievement. By designing a system that reinforces success through consistent habits, we free ourselves from the unpredictability of willpower and motivation. Through deliberate practice and environmental design, peak performance becomes an automatic outcome, allowing us to operate at our highest level with efficiency, consistency, and ease.

Chapter 10 Action Items

- Identify and automate essential goal-aligned behaviors. *(Time Commitment: ~1 hour)*
- Develop and implement triggers to connect your desired behaviors. *(Time Commitment: ~30 minutes)*
- Harness your willpower to solidify new habits—this process will take 18 days or more to fully automate. *(Time Commitment: ~30 minutes)*

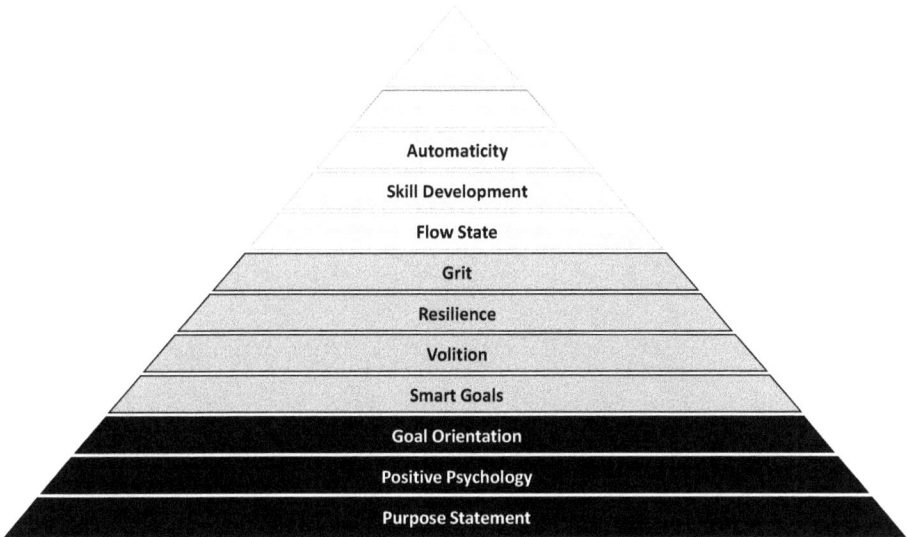

Automaticity
Skill Development
Flow State
Grit
Resilience
Volition
Smart Goals
Goal Orientation
Positive Psychology
Purpose Statement

CHAPTER 11

GOAL-CONGRUENCY

ALIGNING YOUR RESOURCES FOR MAXIMUM SUCCESS

STORY: AN AUDACIOUS FUTURE THROUGH
GOAL-CONGRUENT BEHAVIOR

From an early age, Elon Musk had incredible ambition and wanted to reshape the world. As a child in South Africa, he was an avid reader, consuming entire encyclopedias and teaching himself programming at just 12 years old. He didn't allow his interests to be scattered; they were sharply focused on a singular vision—how technology could push humanity forward. He didn't just dream about change—he systematically aligned every decision he made toward that vision.

At 17, he moved to North America, believing it was the best place to pursue his ambitions. Unlike many who chase status or financial success, Musk chose paths that directly supported his long-term goals. He studied physics and economics, understanding that mastering both would be crucial for solving the world's biggest challenges. He didn't take shortcuts or get sidetracked by conventional careers. Every move he made served his overarching mission of advancing human progress through technology.

When he co-founded Zip2, a software company that helped newspapers transition into the digital age, it wasn't about getting rich. It was about building foundational knowledge and capital for bigger goals. After selling Zip2, he could have retired comfortably, but instead, he immediately funneled his resources into his next ventures: PayPal, Tesla, and SpaceX. The money wasn't the goal—advancing electric vehicles and space travel was.

SpaceX is perhaps the most striking example of goal-congruency in action. While others saw commercial space travel as an impossible endeavor, Musk saw a necessity. NASA was reducing its missions, and no private companies were seriously attempting interplanetary travel. Musk did not have a specific background in rocketry, but that was rectified by devouring textbooks, hiring the best minds in aerospace, and immersing himself in the field. He didn't dabble in side projects or hedge his bets. Every decision, every hour of his day, was dedicated to solving the specific problem of making space travel viable.

When SpaceX nearly collapsed after three failed rocket launches, most entrepreneurs would have pivoted to something safer. Musk doubled down. He invested his last remaining funds, ensuring that the fourth launch was successful. Had he spread his focus or chosen a more comfortable route, SpaceX would have never made history as the first private company to send a spacecraft to the International Space Station—and for later rescuing two American astronauts stranded on the International Space Station.

Elon Musk's success is an excellent example of the power and importance of goal-congruency. Every major decision in his life has been aligned with his ultimate mission, never sacrificing long-term vision for short-term gain. His story exemplifies how aligning every thought, action, and resource toward a singular goal creates unstoppable momentum. In this chapter, we will explore the art of intentionally directing our energy and resources toward goal-congruent behavior, ensuring every effort propels us closer to our success.

DEFINITION OF GOAL-CONGRUENT BEHAVIOR

Goal-congruent behavior is the deliberate alignment of one's actions with one's overarching aspirations, ensuring that one's daily effort contributes meaningfully toward long-term success. Unlike general good habits, which may lead to positive outcomes over time, goal-congruent behavior is highly intentional and strategic. It is not just about engaging in productive routines but about ensuring that those routines are directly in service of a clearly defined goal. This alignment eliminates wasted effort, maximizes efficiency, and reduces the internal friction that arises when actions and ambitions are misaligned.

The distinction between good habits and goal-congruent behavior is crucial. Good habits alone, such as exercising regularly or waking up early, are generally beneficial but do not necessarily ensure progress toward a specific objective. Goal-congruent behavior, on the other hand, requires a disciplined focus on actions that directly propel one toward their aspirations. For example, an aspiring entrepreneur might develop the habit of reading business books, but unless they apply that knowledge to building their service, the habit itself does not guarantee goal attainment. True goal-congruency demands the elimination of distractions, the efficient use of finite cognitive and physical resources, and a relentless commitment to staying on course toward your long-term goal.

One of the greatest threats to goal-congruent behavior is the temptation to shift focus toward unrelated tasks or pursue short-term gratification over long-term achievement. Mental distractions, competing priorities, and the illusion of productivity can derail even the most determined individuals. To counteract this, goal-congruent individuals cultivate intense mental focus and demonstrate grit and resilience, mitigating any diversion of their energy to projects or activities that do not serve their ultimate purpose. They do not abandon their efforts at the first sign of difficulty nor allow momentary interests to pull them away from their trajectory.

By practicing goal-congruent behavior, individuals create a self-reinforcing cycle of motivation and achievement. Each step forward strengthens their commitment, reinforcing the belief that success is possible and within their control. This psychological alignment not only increases efficiency but also fosters deep satisfaction, as progress toward meaningful goals enhances overall well-being through the achievement of meaningful milestones. In contrast, misalignment between daily actions and long-term aspirations leads to frustration, self-doubt, and burnout.[34]

Ultimately, goal-congruent behavior is about engineering one's daily behaviors for success. It is a methodical approach that prioritizes purposeful action, minimizes distractions, and ensures that every effort contributes to a unified vision. When properly applied, this construct becomes a powerful mechanism for turning ambition into achievement, allowing individuals to reach extraordinary levels of performance over time by maintaining clarity, consistency, and momentum of effort.

THE IMPORTANCE OF GOAL-CONGRUENT BEHAVIOR FOR PEAK PERFORMANCE

Working hard does not mean we will reach our desired destination. Rather, successful goal obtainment is the result of working hard in the right direction. Many people expend immense energy, push through exhaustion, and sacrifice their time, only to find themselves far from where they originally intended to go. The problem is not a lack of effort, but a lack of alignment between their daily actions and their long-term goals. Goal-congruent behavior ensures that every ounce of energy, every decision, and every task moves us meaningfully in the direction we want to go. Without this alignment, we risk falling into the trap of pseudo-work—activity that feels productive but ultimately fails to yield real progress.[35]

Pseudo-work is one of the most deceptive obstacles to peak performance. It gives the illusion of diligence, yet it is often filled with tasks that are tangential or unrelated to true goal attainment. Checking emails repeatedly, tweaking minor details, or constantly shifting focus between projects may feel like necessary work, but these behaviors drain valuable cognitive resources without driving real results. In contrast, goal-congruent behavior channels effort into high-impact actions that directly contribute to success. It cuts through distractions, allowing us to focus on what truly matters rather than what merely feels urgent.

Emotional decision-making is another pitfall that can derail peak performance. When we lack clarity of purpose, we become reactive rather than strategic, making choices based on immediate feelings rather than long-term objectives. This often leads to inconsistency—working tirelessly one day and losing momentum the next. Without intentional alignment, emotions dictate our actions, leading to burnout, frustration, and a cycle of starting over. Goal-congruent individuals, however, do not leave their success to chance. They replace emotional spontaneity and procrastination with structured, purposeful planning, ensuring that their actions remain consistent regardless of temporary feelings or external pressures or comparisons.[36]

By minimizing pseudo-work and emotional decision-making, goal-congruent behavior fosters efficiency and progress. It transforms the exhausting grind of scattered effort into a streamlined, strategic pursuit of excellence. Every task becomes a stepping stone toward a meaningful objective, every habit serves a purpose, and every decision is made with clarity and intent. This alignment not only accelerates achievement but also sustains motivation, as measurable progress reinforces a sense of purpose and direction.

Peak performance is not about doing more—it is about doing what matters most, with relentless focus and precision. Goal-congruent behavior is the key to unlocking this level of success. It ensures that the work we do is not just hard, but effective, bringing us closer to our ultimate aspirations rather than leading us astray. By committing to purposeful action and eliminating wasted effort, we create a direct path to extraordinary achievement.

EFFECTIVELY DEVELOPING GOAL-CONGRUENT BEHAVIOR FOR PEAK PERFORMANCE

Achieving peak performance requires aligning your effort with your purpose. Goal-congruent behavior ensures that each action, habit, and decision contribute to long-term objectives, creating a path to your success. By intentionally designing our daily efforts to align with our priorities, we maximize efficiency, maintain motivation, and experience greater well-being. The following key strategies will help establish and sustain goal-congruent behavior for peak performance:

Step 1. Be Clear about Your Goals

Before aligning daily actions, you must first define your destination. Clarity on both short-term and long-term goals is essential to ensure that every effort contributes meaningfully. Goals should be specific, measurable, and purpose-driven, allowing you to notice and then filter out distractions and focus only on actions that take you where you want to go. When your objectives are well-defined, decision-making becomes more strategic, reducing wasted effort and ensuring that your time and energy are invested wisely. Recognizing when an action is not goal-congruent is just as important as recognizing when it is.

Step 2. Ensure Your Daily Efforts Align with Long-Term Objectives

Once your primary goals are established, the next step is aligning daily efforts with them. Many people fall into the trap of working hard on tasks that provide little or no forward momentum, yet feel very effortful. To ensure congruency, frequently ask yourself: *Is this action bringing me closer to my ultimate goal?* If not, reevaluate and redirect efforts toward tasks that create real progress. Structuring your day around goal-aligned priorities enhances productivity and prevents the inefficiency of scattered effort.

Step 3. Create Positive Habits that Support Your Goals

Habits shape our behaviors and ultimately define our trajectory. By cultivating positive, goal-congruent habits, we automate success, reducing our dependence on willpower for constant decision-making. Fortunately, it is the small, consistent actions—repeated over time—that lead to extraordinary results. For instance, if your goal is to become an industry expert, dedicating daily time to focused reading and skill development ensures steady progress. By embedding goal-supporting behaviors into daily routines, success becomes a natural byproduct rather than a struggle through conscious effort. Over time, these habits accumulate, often leading to remarkable progress before we even realize the extent of our achievements.

Step 4. Design Cues to Trigger Goal-Congruent Behavior

External and internal cues play a crucial role in reinforcing our new goal-aligned actions. Creating intentional triggers—such as setting a morning time to prioritize deep work or using obvious cues like lunch or arriving home from work—keeps your goals at the forefront of your mind as each day unfolds. These cues minimize reliance on willpower, making goal-congruent actions automatic and effortless. By strategically designing an environment that nudges you toward desired behaviors, you eliminate friction and increase consistency.

The following are five common cues that you may find useful to initiate flow and goal-congruent behavior:

- **Time-Based Cues** – Scheduling deep work, workouts, or skill-building at the same time each day helps train the brain to associate that time with focused effort. (e.g., Writers like to start writing at the same early morning hour daily.)[22]
- **Location-Based Cues** – Associating specific places with certain activities reinforces goal alignment. (e.g., A well-organized workspace signals focus, while setting out workout gear in advance cues exercise.)[31]
- **Pre-Activity Rituals** – Small, repetitive actions before a task helps transition into a peak flow state. (e.g., Athletes may prepare the same way before the beginning of their event to prime their focus.)[37]

- **Sensory Triggers** – Music, scents, or visual cues can reinforce goal-oriented habits. (e.g., Many professionals use a specific playlist or noise level to enter deep work mode.)[31]
- **Emotional or Mental Cues** – Setting an intentional mindset before engaging in an activity reinforces consistency. (e.g., Public speakers may use power poses or breathing techniques to prepare for high-energy performance.)[31]

By intentionally designing your cues, you can reduce friction and make goal-congruent behaviors effortless. These automatic triggers will reinforce your goal-congruent behaviors. The easier it is to start, the more consistent and effective your efforts will become.

Step 5. Ensure Consistency and Eliminate Conflicting Behaviors

Goal-congruent consistency is the backbone of progress. Sporadic effort produces sporadic results, while sustained, effective action leads to mastery and long-term achievement. To maintain consistency, it's essential to critically evaluate how each activity aligns with your goals. Before committing to any task, ask yourself:

- **How much time will this activity require that is not goal-congruent?** If an activity consumes significant time but does not directly support your long-term objectives, reconsider whether it is worth pursuing.
- **Which goal does this activity support?** Clearly identifying how an action contributes to a specific goal prevents wasted effort on unrelated or counterproductive tasks.
- **What percentage of my available working time is being designated for this activity?** If a substantial portion of your time is spent on low-priority tasks, realignment is necessary to maximize efficiency.

Additionally, be mindful of hidden productivity drains, such as distractions, procrastination, or impulsive commitments that consume energy without yielding meaningful progress. Research suggests that high achievers routinely assess their activities to ensure every action moves them closer to their goals rather than scattering their focus. The more stream-lined and intentional your efforts, the faster you will reach milestones.[38]

Periodically evaluating goal-congruency ensures that your actions remain aligned with evolving aspirations. Your purpose statement and long-term goals are not static—they may shift as you gain new insights, develop new skills, or refine your vision for success. Conduct regular self-audits, whether weekly, monthly, or quarterly, to assess whether your current habits, routines, and focus areas are still propelling you forward.

Previously developed habits, even those that once served you well, may become limiting if they no longer contribute to skill growth or if they create a plateau in your development. Ask yourself: *Are my current actions challenging me, or am I simply maintaining the status quo? Have my goals evolved in a way that requires new strategies or behaviors? Are there habits I need to refine, replace, or eliminate to ensure continued progress?* If misalignment is found, adjust accordingly to maintain momentum. This continuous refinement process keeps you agile, ensuring that every effort is an intentional investment in your long-term success.

CHAPTER 11 REFLECTION: HOW GOAL-CONGRUENT BEHAVIOR CREATES PEAK PERFORMANCE

Hard work alone does not guarantee success. Many people exert tremendous effort yet find themselves far from ever reaching their goals. The key difference between effort that leads to achievement and effort that leads to exhaustion is goal-congruency—ensuring that every action aligns with where you ultimately want to be.

One of the greatest threats to goal-congruent behavior is the temptation to shift focus toward unrelated tasks or short-term gratification. Mental distractions, competing priorities, and the illusion of productivity can lead even the most determined individuals astray. Without intentional alignment, it's easy to spend time and energy on tasks that feel productive but fail to move you meaningfully toward your goals.

By implementing the steps outlined in this chapter, you create a framework that supports long-term success. From gaining clarity on your goals to designing intentional cues and eliminating conflicting behaviors, each step builds upon the last to ensure that your daily efforts consistently drive you forward. Goal-congruent behavior isn't just about discipline—it's about creating an environment where success becomes inevitable.

Remember, every 'yes' to one opportunity is a 'no' to another. Thriving in life requires rejecting chaos and short-term distractions so you can confidently say 'yes' to what truly matters. When you fully embrace the power of purposeful choices, you create a pathway for extraordinary achievement—one goal-aligned step at a time.

Chapter 11 Action Items

- Align your daily efforts with your long-term goals—start eliminating behaviors that don't support your objectives. *(Time Commitment: ~1 hour)*
- Ensure the habits from Chapter 10 align with your purpose statement objectives, automating your journey to outlier status. *(Time Commitment: ~30 minutes)*

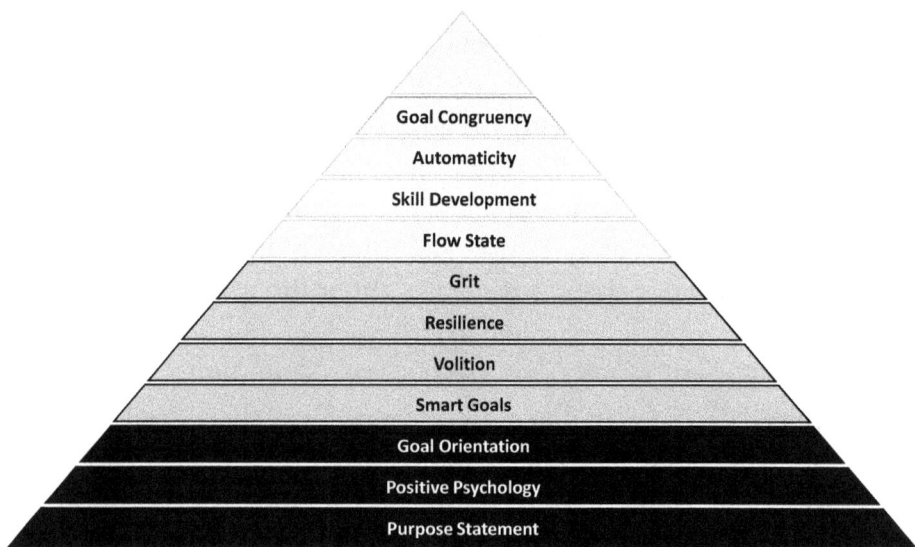

Goal Congruency
Automaticity
Skill Development
Flow State
Grit
Resilience
Volition
Smart Goals
Goal Orientation
Positive Psychology
Purpose Statement

CHAPTER 12

BEING THE BEST

PUSHING PAST AVERAGE TO ACHIEVE EXTRAORDINARY SUCCESS

STORY: FROM HUMBLE BEGINNINGS TO INDUSTRY OUTLIER

Howard Schultz grew up in a working-class housing complex in Brooklyn, New York, where financial struggles were a daily reality. His father held low-wage jobs without benefits, and the instability left a lasting impression on Schultz. From a young age, he knew he wanted something different. He wanted to break free from the cycle of financial hardship.

Determined to change his future, Schultz worked tirelessly to pay his way through Northern Michigan University, becoming the first in his family to attend college. It wasn't easy. He took out loans, worked odd jobs, and pushed through each semester with the knowledge that education could open doors. But simply earning a degree didn't immediately lead to success. After graduating, Schultz entered the working world like so many others, without status, influence, or financial security.

Schultz's first job after college was selling home appliances for Xerox, where he gained invaluable sales experience. However, he wasn't passionate about it. He wanted more—something that challenged and inspired him. That opportunity came when he joined Hammarplast, a Swedish company that sold kitchen equipment, including coffee makers.

It was in this role that Schultz first encountered Starbucks, a small Seattle-based company that ordered an unusually high number of coffee makers. Intrigued, he flew to Seattle in 1981 to see what made this little coffee company different. Starbucks, at this time, was nothing like the global empire we know today. It sold only whole coffee beans and equipment. There was no brewed coffee, no baristas, and no café experience. Yet, Schultz saw something special.

Impressed by Starbucks' passion for quality coffee, he convinced its owners to hire him as director of retail operations and marketing. At the time, Starbucks had just four stores. Schultz wasn't joining a powerhouse brand. He was stepping into a small, niche business with no guarantee of success. But he took the risk, eager to learn the industry from the inside out.

As Schultz worked at Starbucks, he saw untapped potential. A business trip to Italy in 1983 was a turning point. He became fascinated by the espresso bar culture in Milan, where cafes weren't just about coffee but about community and experience. Schultz envisioned bringing this model to America. He pitched the idea to Starbucks' owners, but they rejected it, unwilling to shift from their bean-selling business model to that of selling espresso beverages.

Undeterred, Schultz made another bold move by leaving Starbucks to start his own coffee company, Il Giornale, where he could prove his vision. The road wasn't easy. Schultz needed funding, and over 200 investors turned him down. Most people didn't believe Americans would pay premium prices for a coffee experience. The rejections were relentless, but Schultz refused to give up.

Eventually, he secured enough funding to open his first Il Giornale café. The concept worked. People embraced the idea of a coffeehouse as a "third place" between home and work. Schultz demonstrated that his model wasn't just a dream. It was a viable business. In 1987, when the original Starbucks owners decided to sell, Schultz bought the company and merged it with Il Giornale.

Schultz didn't just work his way up. He relentlessly expanded his skillset, built a deep understanding of the coffee industry, and took calculated risks where others hesitated. His journey—from a modest upbringing to running a multi-billion-dollar company—wasn't about luck. It was about learning, adapting, and persistently moving forward.

Over the next several decades, Schultz led Starbucks to global dominance, growing it from a handful of stores to tens of thousands worldwide. He built a brand that wasn't just about coffee but about experience, consistency, and culture. His leadership transformed Starbucks into a household name, making him an outlier in the world of business.

Howard Schultz's story is proof that persistence, vision, and continuous learning are what separates the average from the extraordinary. He didn't start out wealthy or connected. He worked, learned, and refined his approach until he was able to create something exceptional. His journey exemplifies what it means to move beyond the average, to push past mediocrity, and to become a true outlier.

DEFINITION OF BEING AN OUTLIER

To understand what it truly means to be the best, we must first define what it means to stand out. Using statistics, a standard deviation is an objective measurement of how an event deviates from the average in a normal distribution. Statistically, 68% of all values fall within one standard deviation of the average. This means that to be one standard deviation better than the average, you must actually perform at the 84th percentile relative to your peers (68% of the inner quartile of performance as well as the 16% of the bottom quartile performers).

At first glance, this may seem like an attainable goal. However, by definition, most people will not achieve it. The challenge is compounded by the fact that many individuals overestimate their abilities due to ego protection or superiority bias—the tendency to perceive oneself as above average despite objective evidence suggesting otherwise. This cognitive bias often leads people to assume they are performing at a higher level than they actually are. Furthermore, one's performance must consistently fall outside the average curve.

To reliably be one standard deviation above your peer group, you must demonstrate exceptional proficiency, competence, or talent in your field. This means possessing a deeper understanding of the subject matter, excelling in a particular skill, or showcasing advanced ability and knowledge. More importantly, high performance must be consistent; one exceptional moment does not define excellence—sustained achievement does. Thus, being in the 84th percentile sets you apart, indicating that your expertise, problem-solving ability, and execution surpass those of the vast majority in your field. Achieving this level of competence requires deliberate effort, continuous learning, and a commitment to refining your skills beyond what is required.

Ultimately, achieving excellence requires a blend of self-efficacy and consistent, measurable performance that sets you apart from the majority. To become an outlier, you must be prepared to invest the effort needed to surpass the average and attain truly exceptional results. Those who reach this level of expertise are often recognized and valued for their contributions, creating opportunities for leadership, influence, and greater success.[39]

The Importance of Being an Outlier for Peak Performance

Becoming an outlier in your field is critical for achieving peak performance. Those who acquire exceptional skills and continuously refine them not only stand out but also consistently perform at the highest level, allowing for sustained, superior performance that differentiates them from the majority. To reach this level, lifelong skill development is essential. Mastering relevant career skills and continually expanding your expertise ensures that you remain competitive and indispensable. Your increased competence will set you apart, leading to greater recognition, career advancement, and financial rewards. Promotions, raises, and leadership opportunities often follow those who can perform at a level beyond their peers.

Some key areas for skill development according to research on employable skills include:[40]

- **Job-Specific Expertise:** Mastery of technical and professional skills unique to your field.
- **Tools and Technologies:** Proficiency in industry-relevant tools, software, and systems.
- **Organizational Knowledge:** Deep understanding of company-specific processes and best practices.

- **Communication and Teamwork:** The ability to collaborate effectively, articulate ideas, and lead initiatives.
- **Personal Management:** Resilience, time management, and adaptability to navigate professional challenges.

The true value of being an outlier becomes evident when complex, high-stakes challenges arise within your environment. While others struggle, you will possess the skills necessary to handle demanding tasks with precision and efficiency. Your ability to deliver solutions where others fall short time and time again will reinforce your reputation as a top performer, securing your place as a trusted expert within your organization.

This research also points to three general categories of essential skills for career success: *academic skills, personal management skills,* and *teamwork skills.*[40]

- **Academic Skills:** The technical and intellectual foundation required to execute job tasks effectively. This includes knowledge of tools, language, and specialized industry concepts.
- **Personal Management Skills:** Attributes that influence work ethic, problem-solving abilities, and resilience, all of which impact professional success.
- **Teamwork Skills:** The ability to collaborate, build relationships, and drive projects forward in a team-based environment.

While excelling in all three areas is ideal, certain aspects may require targeted development at different career stages. The key is to embrace lifelong skill development—continuously refining your abilities to ensure long-term career growth. The pursuit of mastery is what elevates an individual from average to exceptional, making peak performance a defining character-istic rather than a brief achievement.

In the end, being an outlier requires intentional effort, ongoing improvement, and the ability to perform at a level that sets you apart. If you commit to this mindset, you will not only achieve peak performance but also unlock opportunities that others simply cannot reach.

EFFECTIVELY BECOMING YOUR BEST FOR PEAK PERFORMANCE

Becoming the best in your field requires consistent excellence, superior skills, and a deep understanding of your discipline. Achieving exceptional proficiency allows you to stand out, nat-urally earn recognition, and unlock career advancements such as promotions and financial rewards. This high level of success will have nothing to do with luck; it will be the result of inten-tional effort, continuous learning, and strategic development.

To effectively become your best and achieve peak performance, follow these essential steps:

Step 1. Apply Your Skills to Real-World Challenges

Passive learning is not enough. Actively seek hands-on expe-rience by engaging in projects, tasks, and responsibilities that challenge and stretch your abilities. Take on high-impact assignments that allow you to develop job-specific skills, tech-nology proficiency, and organizational expertise.

At first, your skills may be inadequate, leading to aver-age or even "needs improvement" reviews. While this can be uncomfortable, it's a natural part of the growth process. Rather than avoiding challenges where you might struggle, use these experiences to identify areas that need improvement and acquire the necessary training. Growth comes from embracing discomfort and building new competencies, not from playing it safe. While it's important to recognize your limits for safety, habitually avoiding challenges where failure is possible ensures that your progress will stagnate indefinitely. The more you apply your knowledge in real situations, the more feedback you will gather about your skills. Over time, you will refine and improve your skills significantly.

Step 2. Learn from the Best

Identify individuals who excel in your field and study their methods, techniques, and work habits. Whether through direct mentorship, observation, or analyzing their work, seek to understand what makes them exceptional. This could include their decision-making process, problem-solving techniques, or ability to handle high-pressure situations. Consider reaching out to them to learn about the training or processes they find most useful. Model your performance after these successful examples, adapting their strategies to fit your strengths and career path. You don't have to exactly mirror them, but there are likely a few key principles that contribute to their success that you could incorporate into your daily routine.

Step 3. Compare and Identify Gaps against Industry Standards

To improve, you must first understand where you currently stand against quantifiable standards. Use objective benchmarks, performance metrics, or self-assessments to compare your abilities with high performers in your field. Identify skill gaps and areas where your performance falls short, then create a plan to close those gaps through focused learning and practice.

Self-assessment alone can be misleading due to flawed self-assessment and superiority bias—the tendency to make excuses for ourselves while also overestimating our own abilities. To combat this, actively seek feedback from supervisors, mentors, and peers. Constructive criticism provides clarity on your weaknesses and helps you make targeted improvements. Regularly evaluate your progress and adjust your strategies accordingly.[28]

Finally, create SMART goals to guide your skill development in these areas. Break these goals into smaller, actionable steps that can be integrated into your daily and weekly routine. Improvement requires grit and patience. However, over time, this structured approach will yield significant performance improvements.[22]

Step 4. Adapt, Improve, and Embrace Lifelong Skill Development

Bringing out your best requires a strategy of continuous improvement. As you strive for growth, be willing to adapt your methods, learn new techniques, and refine your approach based on feedback and milestone achievements. Flexibility is key to sustaining progress, keeping you aligned with evolving industry demands and shifting responsibilities. Setbacks are inevitable, but rather than viewing them as failures, treat them as valuable learning opportunities that refine your skills and strengthen your resilience.

Becoming the best is a lifelong commitment, built on a foundation of continuous learning and persistent effort. Seek out new challenges, stay informed about industry advancements, and regularly push beyond your comfort zone. True outliers distinguish themselves through their ability to persevere, learn, and evolve. By combining adaptability with a commitment to lifelong learning, you create a powerful approach to both personal and professional success—one that keeps you innovative, resilient, and always moving forward.

Chapter 12 Reflection: How Being Your Best Creates Peak Performance

While many would celebrate being marginally better than average, achieving peak performance is about consistently setting yourself well apart through superior skill, knowledge, and execution. To truly be one standard deviation above the average, you must operate at the 84th percentile, regularly outperforming the majority of your peer group. This requires more than just effort; it demands self-efficacy, intentional skill development, and a track record of measurable success.

Throughout this chapter, we have explored the essential components of becoming an outlier in your field and how sustained improvement leads to excellence. Career growth, recognition, and long-term success are built upon the mastery of specialized expertise, proficiency in industry-relevant tools and technologies, and a deep understanding of organizational processes. Beyond technical skills, true distinction comes from the ability to communicate effectively, collaborate seamlessly, and lead with clarity and confidence. Just as crucial is personal management—the resilience to navigate challenges and distractions, the discipline to refine your craft, and the adaptability to evolve in an ever-changing professional landscape.

Becoming your best is not a passive process but an intentional and ongoing commitment to improvement. The journey toward excellence requires actively applying your skills in real-world situations, observing and learning from the best in your field, and consistently measuring your performance against industry benchmarks. Progress comes from a willingness to refine your approach, seek meaningful feedback, and adapt to emerging challenges. Mastery is a continuous pursuit that requires the courage to push beyond comfort zones and embrace a mindset of lifelong development.

By combining these steps and maintaining a relentless focus on growth, you will consistently perform at the highest level in your career. True success does not come from a single moment of achievement but from sustained excellence, continuous improvement, and a mindset of mastery. Becoming your best is a journey—one that, when pursued with purpose and dedication, leads to lasting impact, recognition, and extraordinary success.

CHAPTER 12 ACTION ITEMS

- Identify areas where your skills need improvement. *(Time Commitment: ~1 hour)*
- Develop an action plan to enhance your skills, apply your learning to real-world projects, and then objectively evaluate your effectiveness. *(Time Commitment: ~1 hour)*
- Commit to this continuous skill development throughout your life. *(Always)*

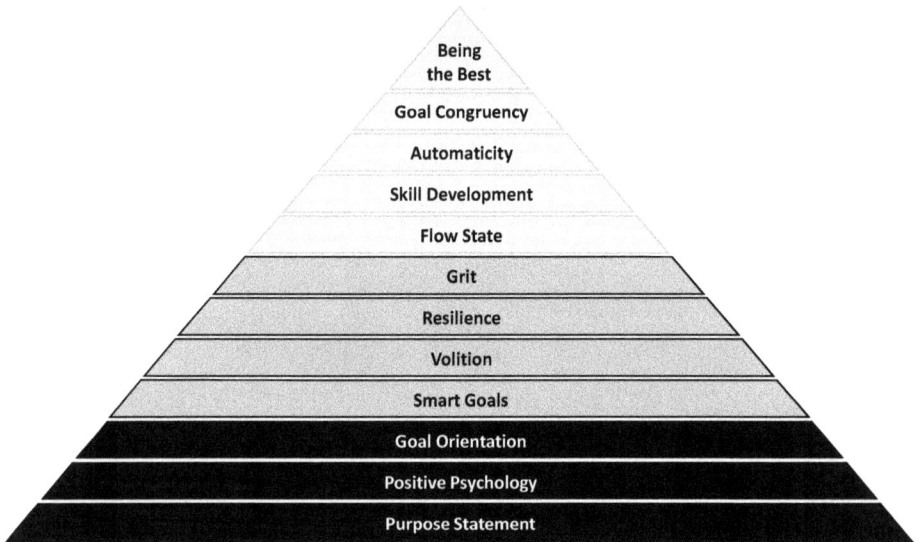

Being
the Best

Goal Congruency

Automaticity

Skill Development

Flow State

Grit

Resilience

Volition

Smart Goals

Goal Orientation

Positive Psychology

Purpose Statement

YOUR STORY

It has been my great pleasure to present these psychological constructs to you as you continue developing your skills in pursuit of consistent peak performance. As you read the inspiring stories of those who have harnessed these principles, I hope you've begun to see just how far they can take you. Now, the question is: What will your story be?

While learning from others is invaluable, your journey will be uniquely shaped by your context, aspirations, and the challenges you overcome. Who knows what remarkable contributions you will make? As you grow, I encourage you to do so in a way that radiates outward. First, cultivate exceptional well-being in your own life, building deep reserves of self-regulation that will empower you to help others. Then, enrich your family by fostering positivity, encouragement, and strong relationships. Finally, with a solid foundation, you will be positioned to make a lasting impact on your organization, your community, and beyond—leaving the world better through your talents, discipline, and unwavering pursuit of excellence. It is in serving others that we find our most meaningful contributions, using the abilities God has given us to make the most of this one life.

Remember, you can always revisit these psychological constructs often when you need to enhance them. Be careful not to underestimate the profound impact a blind spot can have on your journey though. For instance, the very first chapter—developing a purpose statement—is often overlooked. Yet, without taking the time to truly identify our strengths and define our purpose, we risk years of effort spent chasing goals that were never deeply meaningful to us. That realization, often arriving later in life, can be devastating to our well-being. If you find yourself in this difficult situation, draw on resilience to recalibrate your path, align your pursuits with your true purpose, and start again.

Another critical oversight is the tendency to default to a performance-approach goal orientation rather than a mastery-approach. Many highly driven individuals instinctively seek external validation, pushing themselves—and those around them—to the brink in pursuit of measurable achievements. While this approach may yield short-term success, it comes at a steep cost: strained relationships, chronic anxiety, declining mental and physical health, and an ever-present risk of quitting. In contrast, a mastery-approach orientation fosters the same high levels of achievement but with continuous growth, innovation, and sustainable excellence—without the destructive trade-offs. Though shifting mindsets from performance to mastery may feel challenging at the moment, over the long run, mastery-oriented individuals consistently surpass those who are solely driven by performance.

Now, I invite you to go forward and commit to lifelong skill development. Ensure that your daily actions are goal congruent. Embrace failure as required stepping stones, stretching yourself to become an outlier in your field. I am rooting for you. I believe in you. Go and be extraordinary with the one life God has given you.

I truly hope to hear how you've elevated your own well-being, enriched your family, and made meaningful contributions to your community—all by operating at your peak performance.

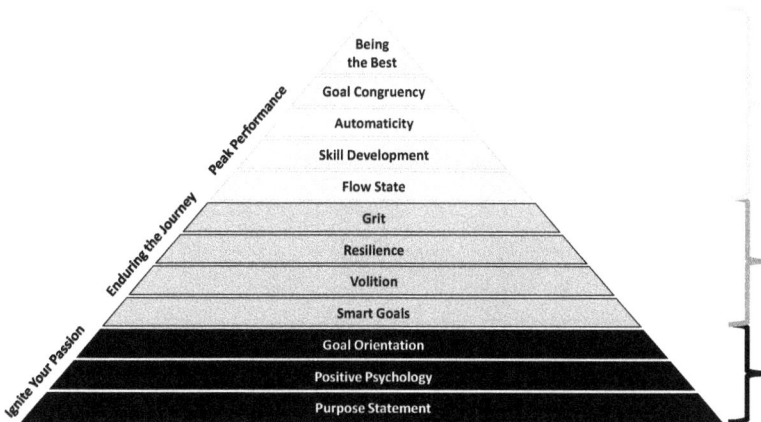

Being
the Best

Goal Congruency

Automaticity

Skill Development

Flow State

Grit

Resilience

Volition

Smart Goals

Goal Orientation

Positive Psychology

Purpose Statement

Peak Performance

Enduring the Journey

Ignite Your Passion

These principles
transform you from
great to truly
exceptional.

These principles fuel
your long journey to
meaningful
contribution.

Neglecting these
principles results in
perpetually
restarting.

REFERENCES

1. Bouchrika, I. (2024, December 10). *College dropout rates: 2024 statistics by race, gender & income*. Research.com. https://research.com/universities-colleges/college-dropout-rates

2. Revankar, S. (2024, October 9). *Career change statistics by demographics, job tenure, seniority level insights, income insights, job satisfaction and facts*. Sci-Tech Today. https://www.sci-tech-today.com/stats/career-change-statistics/

3. Layard, R. (2011, May 14). *Flourish: A new understanding of happiness and well-being - and how to achieve them by Martin Seligman – Review*. The Guardian. https://www.theguardian.com/science/2011/may/15/flourish-science-of-happiness-psychology-review

4. Seligman, M. E. (2004). Authentic happiness: Using the new positive psychology to realize your potential for lasting fulfillment. Simon and Schuster.

5. Seligman, M. (2018). PERMA and the building blocks of well-being. *The journal of positive psychology*, *13*(4), 333–5.

6. Seligman, M.E. (2011). *Flourish: A visionary new understanding of happiness and well-being*. Simon and Schuster.

7. Csikszentmihalyi, M. (1990). Flow: The psychology of optimal experience. Harper & Row.

8. Fredrickson, B.L. (2004). The broaden–and–build theory of positive emotions. *Philosophical transactions of the royal society of London. Series B: Biological Sciences*, *359*(1449), 1367–77.

9. Seligman, M. E. P. (2006). Learned optimism: How to change your mind and your life. Vintage Books.

10. Fredrickson, B.L., & Losada, M.F. (2005). Positive affect and the complex dynamics of human flourishing. *American psychologist*, *60*(7),678.

11. Gable, S.L., Gonzaga, G.C., & Strachman, A. (2006). Will you be there for me when things go right? Supportive responses to positive event disclosures. *Journal of personality and social psychology*, *91*(5),904.

12. Locke, E.A., & Latham, G.P. (2019). The development of goal setting theory: A half century retrospective. *Motivation Science*, 5(2),93.

13. Claro, S., Paunesku, D., & Dweck, C.S. (2016). Growth mindset tempers the effects of poverty on academic achievement. *Proceedings of the National Academy of Sciences*, 113(31),8664–8.

14. University of Pennsylvania. (2025). Authentic Happiness. Retrieved April 12, 2025, from https://www.authentichappiness.sas.upenn.edu/

15. Fredrickson, B. L. (2001). The role of positive emotions in positive psychology: The broaden-and-build theory of positive emotions. American Psychologist, 56(3), 218-226.

16. Datu, J.A., Labarda, C.E, & Salanga, M.G. (2020). Flourishing is associated with achievement goal orientations and academic delay of gratification in a collectivist context. *Journal of Happiness Studies*, 21(4),1171–82.

17. Katz-Vago, I., & Benita, M. (2024). Mastery-approach and performance-approach goals predict distinct outcomes during personal academic goal pursuit. *British Journal of Educational Psychology*, 94(2),309–27.

18. Rosen, C.C., Dimotakis, N., Cole, M.S., Taylor, S.G., Simon, L.S., Smith, T.A., & Reina, C.S. (2020). When challenges hinder: An investigation of when and how challenge stressors impact employee outcomes. *Journal of Applied Psychology*, 105(10),1181.

19. Dweck, C. S. (2006). Mindset: The new psychology of success. Random House.

20. Duckworth, A. (2016). *Grit: The power of passion and perseverance*. Scribner.

21. Keller, J.M. (2008). An integrative theory of motivation, volition, and performance. *Technology, Instruction, Cognition, and Learning*, 6(2),79–104.

22. Locke, E. A., & Latham, G. P. (2002). Building a practically useful theory of goal setting and task motivation: A 35-year odyssey. American Psychologist, 57(9), 705-717.

23. Pychyl, T.A. (2013). *Solving the procrastination puzzle: A concise guide to strategies for change*. TarcherPerigee.

24. Duckworth, A. L., Peterson, C., Matthews, M. D., & Kelly, D. R. (2007). Grit: Perseverance and passion for long-term goals. Journal of Personality and Social Psychology, 92(6), 1087-1101.

25. Seligman, M. E. P. (2011). Building resilience. Harvard Business Review. Retrieved April 12, 2025, from https://hbr.org/2011/04/building-resilience

26. Aliyas, S.E., Chalapathy, C.V., Mathew, L., & Thomas, A. (2024). Emotion Regulation and Sports Performance: A Systematic Review. *Journal of Chemical Health Risks*, 14(5),6355.

27. Gold, J., & Ciorciari, J. (2020). A review on the role of the neuroscience of flow states in the modern world. *Behavioral Sciences*, 10(9),137.

28. Andrade, H. L. (2019). A critical review of research on student self-assessment. Frontiers in Education, 4, Article 87. Retrieved April 12, 2025, from https://www.frontiersin.org/articles/10.3389/feduc.2019.00087/full

29. Ericsson, K.A., & Charness, N. (1994). Expert performance: Its structure and acquisition. *American psychologist*, 49(8),725.

30. Wood, W. (2019). *Good habits, bad habits: The science of making positive changes that stick*. Macmillan.

31. Wood, W., & Rünger, D. (2016). Psychology of habit. Annual Review of Psychology, 67, 289-314.

32. Lally, P., Wardle, J., & Gardner, B. (2011). Experiences of habit formation: a qualitative study. *Psychology, Health & Medicine*, 16(4), 484–9.

33. Lally, P., Van Jaarsveld, C.H., Potts, H.W., & Wardle, J. (2010). How are habits formed: Modelling habit formation in the real world. *European journal of social psychology*, 40(6),998–1009.

34. Sirgy, M.J. (2021). Effects of Goals on Wellbeing. In *The Psychology of Quality of Life: Wellbeing and Positive Mental Health*, (pp. 283–305). Cham: Springer International Publishing.

35. Flinchbaugh, C., Luth, M.T., & Li, P. (2015). A challenge or a hindrance? Understanding the effects of stressors and thriving on life satisfaction. *International Journal of Stress Management*, 22(4),323.

36. Sirois, F., & Pychyl, T. (2013). Procrastination and the priority of short-term mood regulation: Consequences for future self. *Social and personality psychology compass*, 7(2),115–27.

37. Hagan Jnr, J. E., & Schack, T. (2019). Integrating pre-game rituals and pre-performance routines in a culture-specific context: Implications for sport psychology consultancy. International Journal of Sport and Exercise Psychology, 17(1), 18-31.

38. Erez, A., Judge, T.A. (2001). Relationship of core self-evaluations to goal setting, motivation, and performance. *Journal of applied psychology*, 86(6):1270.

39. Terry, R. P., McGee, J. E., Kass, M. J., & Collings, D. G. (2023). Assessing star value: The influence of prior performance and visibility on compensation strategy. Human Resource Management Journal, 33(2), 307-327.

40. Bloom, M. R., & Kitagawa, K. G. (1999). Understanding employability skills. *Conference Board of Canada*.

ABOUT THE AUTHOR

With the unpredictability of life, one truth remains: your attitude and your work ethic are within your control. Jason embraced this reality early on, channeling his focus and commitment to outwork others to achieve success. Yet, despite relentless passion and effort, he found himself unable to surpass the best. This realization sparked an insatiable curiosity to master the science of goal achievement and uncover the hidden ingredients required for peak performance.

Equipped with the analytical rigor of an engineering degree, the strategic acumen of a business degree, the tactical insights of a coach, and the expert understanding of human psychology gained through his doctorate, Jason embarked on a journey of discovery. He explored, researched, and applied the principles of psychology to uncover key constructs that shape extraordinary success and life outcomes.

A defining moment in his pursuit came during a private conversation with world champion boxer Evander Holyfield. When Jason asked what separates someone who gives their very best, but finishes second from the champion, Holyfield's response was simple, yet profound: "God is never going to hold someone else back so that you can win." This truth reframed Jason's understanding of success—there is more to achievement than just effort.

Through this lens, Jason has dedicated his career to equipping others with tools grounded in rigorous psychological research to unlock their highest performance. Whether you're a leader, coach, employee, athlete, or student, these evidence-based principles empower you to address blind spots, align your actions with your ambitions, and achieve outcomes you once thought impossible.

Wherever you are in your journey, the research-backed strategies presented in this book will guide you to make the adjustments necessary to reach your peak and live an extraordinary life. By applying these researched principles, you will undoubtedly experience tremendous progress toward your ambitions.

TREMENDOUS LIFE TIP

You'll be the <u>same person</u> five
years from now that you are
today <u>except</u> for two things:
the people you meet
and *the books you read*.

CHARLIE "TREMENDOUS" JONES

www.ingramcontent.com/pod-product-compliance
Lightning Source LLC
Chambersburg PA
CBHW051421090426
42737CB00014B/2774